Creating Development Environments with Vagrant

Second Edition

Leverage the power of Vagrant to create and manage virtual development environments with Puppet, Chef, and VirtualBox

Michael Peacock

BIRMINGHAM - MUMBAI

Creating Development Environments with Vagrant

Second Edition

Copyright © 2015 Packt Publishing

All rights reserved. No part of this book may be reproduced, stored in a retrieval system, or transmitted in any form or by any means, without the prior written permission of the publisher, except in the case of brief quotations embedded in critical articles or reviews.

Every effort has been made in the preparation of this book to ensure the accuracy of the information presented. However, the information contained in this book is sold without warranty, either express or implied. Neither the author, nor Packt Publishing, and its dealers and distributors will be held liable for any damages caused or alleged to be caused directly or indirectly by this book.

Packt Publishing has endeavored to provide trademark information about all of the companies and products mentioned in this book by the appropriate use of capitals. However, Packt Publishing cannot guarantee the accuracy of this information.

First published: August 2013

Second edition: March 2015

Production reference: 1050315

Published by Packt Publishing Ltd.
Livery Place
35 Livery Street
Birmingham B3 2PB, UK.

ISBN 978-1-78439-702-9

www.packtpub.com

Credits

Author
Michael Peacock

Reviewers
Jonathan Bardo
Anirudh Bhatnagar

Commissioning Editor
Usha Iyer

Acquisition Editors
Richard Brookes-Bland
Ellen Bishop

Content Development Editor
Sriram Neelakantan

Technical Editor
Mrunal M. Chavan

Copy Editor
Rashmi Sawant

Project Coordinator
Aboli Ambardekar

Proofreaders
Simran Bhogal
Maria Gould
Paul Hindle

Indexer
Monica Ajmera Mehta

Production Coordinator
Arvindkumar Gupta

Cover Work
Arvindkumar Gupta

About the Author

Michael Peacock is an experienced software developer and team lead from Newcastle, UK, with a degree in software engineering from the University of Durham.

After spending a number of years running his own web agency, and subsequently, working directly for a number of software start-ups, he now runs his own software development agency, working on a range of projects for an array of different clients.

He is the author of *Creating Development Environments with Vagrant*, *PHP 5 Social Networking*, *PHP 5 E-Commerce Development*, *Drupal 7 Social Networking*, and *Selling online with Drupal e-Commerce* and *Building Websites with TYPO3*, all by Packt Publishing. The other publications Michael has been involved in include *Advanced API Security*, *Mobile Web Development*, *Jenkins Continuous Integration Cookbook*, and *Drupal for Education and E-Learning*; for these he acted as a technical reviewer.

Michael has also presented at a number of user groups and technical conferences, including PHP UK Conference, Dutch PHP Conference, ConFoo, PHPNE, PHPNW, and Could Connect Santa Clara.

You can follow Michael on Twitter (@michaelpeacock), or find out more about him through his website (www.michaelpeacock.co.uk).

> I'd like to thank the team at Packt Publishing for their help in getting this revised edition of the book published, and the technical reviewers for ensuring technical accuracy in the book.

About the Reviewers

Jonathan Bardo is a Montreal-based web developer with a keen interest for new technologies and automation. He has worked for many large-scale websites dealing with millions of daily visitors on various platforms. When he is not programming, he likes to watch a good TV show or travel somewhere he has never been before. If you see him riding his motorcycle or skiing down a hill, just say hi! He is very friendly!

Jonathan runs his own consulting company, which lets him meet all sorts of interesting clients, such as Fox Broadcasting (USA), Rogers Digital Media (Canada), and Yellow Pages Group (Canada).

> A special thanks to everyone who has been a part of my journey so far! I wouldn't be here without all the incredible people I worked with everyday.

Anirudh Bhatnagar is a principal consultant at Xebia. He started his career as a developer working in product-based companies such as Adobe.

Anirudh has been working mostly with Java-based technology stacks that use Spring, Hibernate, XML, web services, REST, CMS, SSO, ESB, and Liferay.

During the last few years, Anirudh has been advocating Continuous Delivery and is interested in technologies such as Chef, Puppet, Jenkins, Vagrant, Docker, and many more. He regularly contributes to the community via blogs, articles, meetups, conferences, and open source projects.

More details about him can be found on his blog (`http://anirudhbhatnagar.com`).

www.PacktPub.com

Support files, eBooks, discount offers, and more

For support files and downloads related to your book, please visit `www.PacktPub.com`.

Did you know that Packt offers eBook versions of every book published, with PDF and ePub files available? You can upgrade to the eBook version at `www.PacktPub.com` and as a print book customer, you are entitled to a discount on the eBook copy. Get in touch with us at `service@packtpub.com` for more details.

At `www.PacktPub.com`, you can also read a collection of free technical articles, sign up for a range of free newsletters and receive exclusive discounts and offers on Packt books and eBooks.

https://www2.packtpub.com/books/subscription/packtlib

Do you need instant solutions to your IT questions? PacktLib is Packt's online digital book library. Here, you can search, access, and read Packt's entire library of books.

Why subscribe?

- Fully searchable across every book published by Packt
- Copy and paste, print, and bookmark content
- On demand and accessible via a web browser

Free access for Packt account holders

If you have an account with Packt at `www.PacktPub.com`, you can use this to access PacktLib today and view 9 entirely free books. Simply use your login credentials for immediate access.

Table of Contents

Preface	**1**
Chapter 1: Getting Started with Vagrant	**7**
Introducing Vagrant	**8**
Requirements for Vagrant	**10**
Getting started	**10**
Installing VirtualBox	11
Installing Vagrant	15
Summary	**18**
Chapter 2: Managing Vagrant Boxes and Projects	**19**
Creating our first Vagrant project	**19**
Managing Vagrant-controlled guest machines	**22**
Powering up a Vagrant-controlled virtual machine	23
Suspending a virtual machine	24
Resuming a virtual machine	25
Shutting down a virtual machine	25
Starting from scratch	25
Updating based on Vagrantfile changes	26
Connecting to the virtual machine over SSH	27
Managing integration between host and guest machines	**27**
Port forwarding	27
Synced folders	28
Networking	28
Autorunning commands	**29**
Managing Vagrant boxes	**30**
Adding Vagrant boxes	31
Listing Vagrant boxes	32
Checking for updates	32
Removing Vagrant boxes	32

Repackaging a Vagrant box	33
Updating the current environment's box	33
Too many Vagrants!	**33**
Summary	**34**
Chapter 3: Provisioning with Puppet	**35**
Provisioning	**36**
Puppet	**37**
Creating modules and manifests with Puppet	38
Puppet classes	38
Default Puppet manifests	38
Resources	40
Resource execution ordering	41
The notify, subscribe, and refreshonly parameters	42
Executing resources in stages	43
Installing software	43
Updating our package manager	44
Installing the nginx package	44
Running the nginx service	45
File management	45
Copying a file	45
Creating a symlink	46
Creating folders	47
Creating multiple folders in one go	47
Cron management	48
Running commands	48
Managing users and groups	49
Creating groups	49
Creating users	50
Updating the sudoers file	50
Creating configurable classes	51
Puppet modules	53
Using Puppet to provision servers	53
Summary	**53**
Chapter 4: Using Ansible	**55**
Understanding Ansible	**56**
Installing Ansible	56
Creating an inventory	57
Creating Ansible playbooks	**58**
Modules – what Ansible can do	58
Installing software	59
Updating our package manager	59
Installing the nginx package	59
Running the nginx service	60

Understanding file management	60
Copying a file	60
Creating a symlink	61
Creating folders	62
Managing cron	62
Running commands	63
Managing users and groups	63
Creating groups	63
Creating users	63
Using Ansible roles	63
Using Ansible to provision servers	64
Summary	**66**
Chapter 5: Using Chef	**67**
Knowing about Chef	**68**
Creating cookbooks and recipes with Chef	**68**
Resources – what Chef can do	69
Installing software	69
Updating our package manager	70
Installing the nginx package	70
Running the nginx service	71
Understanding file management	71
Copying a file	71
Creating a symlink	72
Creating folders	73
Creating multiple folders in a single process with looping	73
Managing cron	74
Running commands	74
Managing users and groups	75
Creating groups	75
Creating users	75
Updating the sudoers file	76
Knowing common resource functionalities	76
Using Chef cookbooks	77
Using Chef to provision servers	77
Summary	**77**
Chapter 6: Provisioning Vagrant Machines with Puppet, Ansible, and Chef	**79**
Provisioning within Vagrant	**79**
Provisioning with Puppet on Vagrant	**80**
Using Puppet in standalone mode	80
Puppet provisioning in action	81
Using Puppet in client/server mode	82

Table of Contents

Provisioning with Ansible on Vagrant	**82**
Provisioning with Chef on Vagrant	**83**
Using Chef-solo	84
Using Chef in client/server mode	85
Provisioning with SSH – a recap	**85**
Using multiple provisioners on a single project	**86**
Overriding provisioning via the command line	**86**
Summary	**87**
Chapter 7: Working with Multiple Machines	**89**
Using multiple machines with Vagrant	**90**
Defining multiple virtual machines	90
Connecting to the multiple virtual machines over SSH	**91**
Networking the multiple virtual machines	93
Provisioning the machines separately	95
Destroying a multimachine project	**97**
Summary	**97**
Chapter 8: Creating Your Own Box	**99**
Getting started	**100**
Preparing the VirtualBox machine	**100**
VirtualBox Guest Additions	**106**
Vagrant authentication	**107**
Vagrant user and admin group	107
The sudoers file	107
Insecure public/private key pair	108
Provisioners	**108**
Installing Puppet	109
Installing Chef	109
Cleaning up the VM	**109**
Export	**109**
Summary	**110**
Chapter 9: HashiCorp Atlas	**111**
Discovering boxes	**112**
Installing new boxes	112
Updating existing boxes	113
Checking for outdated boxes	113
Distributing boxes	**114**

Sharing and connecting with Atlas	**116**
Logging Vagrant into Vagrant Cloud	116
Sharing a Vagrant virtual machine over HTTP(S)	117
Sharing and connecting to a Vagrant virtual machine	119
Summary	**120**
Appendix: A Sample LEMP Stack	**121**
Creating the Vagrant project	**121**
Creating the Puppet manifests	**123**
Installing Nginx	123
Installing PHP	125
Installing the MySQL module	**127**
Default manifest	**128**
Installing Nginx and PHP	128
Hostname configuration	128
E-mail sending services	128
MySQL configuration	129
Launching the virtual machine	**131**
Summary	**131**
Index	**133**

Preface

Web-based software projects are increasingly complicated, with a range of different dependencies, requirements, and interlinking components. Swapping between projects, which require different versions of the same software, becomes troublesome. Getting team members up and running on new projects becomes time-consuming.

Vagrant is a powerful tool used to create, manage, and work with virtualized development environments for your projects. By creating a virtual environment for each project, their dependencies and requirements are isolated, they also don't interfere with the software installed on your own machine such as WAMP or MAMP. Colleagues can be up and running on a new project in minutes with a single command. With Vagrant, we can wipe the slate clean if we break our environment and be back up and running in no time.

What this book covers

Chapter 1, *Getting Started with Vagrant*, introduces the concept of virtualization, its importance in the role of the development environment, and walks you through the Vagrant installation process.

Chapter 2, *Managing Vagrant Boxes and Projects*, walks you through creating Vagrant projects, exploring and configuring the Vagrantfile, and working with base boxes.

Chapter 3, *Provisioning with Puppet*, explores Puppet, the provisioning tool, and how to create Puppet manifests to provision a server.

Chapter 4, *Using Ansible*, explores Ansible, the provisioning tool, and how to create Ansible playbooks to provision a server.

Chapter 5, *Using Chef*, explores Chef, the provisioning tool, and how to create Chef recipes to provision a server.

Preface

Chapter 6, *Provisioning Vagrant Machines with Puppet, Ansible, and Chef*, discusses how to use Puppet, Ansible, and Chef within the context of Vagrant to provision development environments.

Chapter 7, *Working with Multiple Machines*, explores using Vagrant to create and manage projects that use multiple virtual machines, which communicate with each other.

Chapter 8, *Creating Your Own Box*, discusses the process of creating your own base box for use within a Vagrant project.

Chapter 9, *HashiCorp Atlas*, walks you through using Vagrant Share to share SSH and HTTP(S) access to a Vagrant-managed machine, and how to use the services provided through the Vagrant Cloud.

Appendix, *A Sample LEMP Stack*, walks you through the process of creating a LEMP server within a new Vagrant project.

What you need for this book

You will need a Windows, OS X, or Linux computer with Vagrant and Oracle VirtualBox installed, although the installation process for these will be discussed in *Chapter 1*, *Getting Started with Vagrant*.

Who this book is for

This book is for software developers, development managers, and technical team leaders who want to have a more efficient, robust, and flexible development environment for their projects and for their team.

Conventions

In this book, you will find a number of styles of text that distinguish between different kinds of information. Here are some examples of these styles, and an explanation of their meaning.

Code words in text, database table names, folder names, filenames, file extensions, pathnames, dummy URLs, user input, and Twitter handles are shown as follows: "After installing Vagrant, we ran the `vagrant` command to check whether it was installed correctly."

A block of code is set as follows:

```
VAGRANTFILE_API_VERSION = "2"
Vagrant.configure(VAGRANTFILE_API_VERSION) do |config|
  config.vm.box = "base"
end
```

When we wish to draw your attention to a particular part of a code block, the relevant lines or items are set in bold:

```
---
- hosts: default
  tasks:
  - name: update apt cache
    apt: update_cache=yes
  - name: ensure nginx is installed
    apt: pkg=nginx state=present
  - name: write the nginx config file
    template: src=nginx-default-site.conf dest=/etc/nginx/sites-available/default.conf
    notify:
    - restart nginx
  - name: ensure nginx is running
    service: name=nginx state=started
  handlers:
    - name: restart nginx
      service: name=nginx state=restarted
```

Any command-line input or output is written as follows:

```
ansible-playbook our-playbook.yml -i our-inventory-file
```

New terms and **important words** are shown in bold. Words that you see on the screen, in menus or dialog boxes for example, appear in the text like this: "Again, on OS X, the first step is to double-click on the **Vagrant.pkg** icon."

> Warnings or important notes appear in a box like this.

> Tips and tricks appear like this.

Reader feedback

Feedback from our readers is always welcome. Let us know what you think about this book—what you liked or may have disliked. Reader feedback is important for us to develop titles that you really get the most out of.

To send us general feedback, simply send an e-mail to feedback@packtpub.com, and mention the book title via the subject of your message.

If there is a topic that you have expertise in and you are interested in either writing or contributing to a book, see our author guide on www.packtpub.com/authors.

Customer support

Now that you are the proud owner of a Packt book, we have a number of things to help you to get the most from your purchase.

Downloading the example code

You can download the example code files for all Packt books you have purchased from your account at http://www.packtpub.com. If you purchased this book elsewhere, you can visit http://www.packtpub.com/support and register to have the files e-mailed directly to you.

Errata

Although we have taken every care to ensure the accuracy of our content, mistakes do happen. If you find a mistake in one of our books—maybe a mistake in the text or the code—we would be grateful if you would report this to us. By doing so, you can save other readers from frustration and help us improve subsequent versions of this book. If you find any errata, please report them by visiting http://www.packtpub.com/submit-errata, selecting your book, clicking on the **errata submission form** link, and entering the details of your errata. Once your errata are verified, your submission will be accepted and the errata will be uploaded on our website, or added to any list of existing errata, under the Errata section of that title. Any existing errata can be viewed by selecting your title from http://www.packtpub.com/support.

Piracy

Piracy of copyright material on the Internet is an ongoing problem across all media. At Packt, we take the protection of our copyright and licenses very seriously. If you come across any illegal copies of our works, in any form, on the Internet, please provide us with the location address or website name immediately so that we can pursue a remedy.

Please contact us at copyright@packtpub.com with a link to the suspected pirated material.

We appreciate your help in protecting our authors, and our ability to bring you valuable content.

Questions

You can contact us at questions@packtpub.com if you are having a problem with any aspect of the book, and we will do our best to address it.

1
Getting Started with Vagrant

Developing modern web-based applications can be complicated!

The technology behind our projects is becoming more advanced and diverse. Where once projects ran with simply a web server, a database, and a set programming language, now we use tools built in a variety of different languages. We use components and dependencies that need to be installed, and their managed versions, and often projects need to run across multiple machines.

Different projects have their own requirements and dependencies, which are often incompatible with one another. A legacy project might require a specific version of PHP or specific versions of extensions for Apache, whereas another project might require a newer version of PHP and running on **Nginx**. Project switching in this scenario is not easy.

Often, we need to work with teams of people, some of which might be using their own equipment, working remotely, and contractors. This requires you to ensure that everyone runs the same development environment, regardless of their own system and its configuration, the infrastructure changes for projects are tracked and made available to the team, and the project setup is fast for new team members.

Combining these three factors and setting up traditional development environments is becoming more difficult, less relevant, and less helpful for developers.

As projects get more complicated, it's also easy for auxiliary configurations to be forgotten about. Background workers, message queues, cron jobs, and multiserver configurations need to be managed, distributed to the entire team, and then when the time comes, applied to the project when it gets deployed into a production environment.

Virtualized development environments can help with this. Instead of having to battle configurations when working on other projects, each project can simply have its own virtualized environment. It can have its own dedicated web server, database server, and the versions of the programming language and other dependencies it needs. Because it is virtualized, it doesn't impact on other projects; just shut it down and boot up the environment for the other project.

With a virtualized environment, the development environments can also mimic the production environment. You don't need to worry about whether something will work when it gets deployed, if it is being developed on a machine with the exact same software configuration. Even if you deploy on a Linux machine but develop on Windows, your virtualized environment can be Linux, running the same distribution as your production environment.

While a virtualized environment makes different projects and their dependencies easier to manage and separate, they are not the easiest of things to configure and manage. They still need to be configured to work with the project in question, which often involves some level of system administration skills, and we need to connect to these environments and work with them. They also, by design, are not very portable. You need to export a large image of the virtualized environment and share that with your colleagues, and keeping that image up to date as projects evolve can be cumbersome. Thankfully, there is a tool that can manage these virtualized environments for us, and provide a simple interface to configure them; an interface that involves storing configurations in simple plain text files, which are easy to share with colleagues, keeping everyone up to date as the project changes. This tool is **Vagrant**.

Introducing Vagrant

Vagrant (`http://www.vagrantup.com/`) is a powerful development tool that lets you manage and support the virtualization of your development environment. Instead of running all your projects locally on your own computer, having to juggle the different requirements and dependencies of each project, Vagrant lets you run each project in its own dedicated virtual environment.

Vagrant provides a command-line interface and a common configuration language that allows you to easily define and control virtual machines that run on your own systems, but which tightly integrate, and also allows you to define how your own machine and the virtual machine interact. This can involve syncing folders such that the project code, which you edit using the IDE on your computer, is synced so that it runs on the Vagrant development environment.

Vagrant uses providers to integrate with the third-party virtualization software, which provides the virtualized machines for our development environment. The default provider is for Oracle **VirtualBox**; however, there are commercial providers to work with VMware Fusion and also plugins for Vagrant to work with Amazon Web Services. The entire configuration is stored in simple plain text files. The Vagrant configuration (**Vagrantfile**), and the configuration that defines how our Vagrant machines are configured (typically **Shell scripts**, **Ansible playbooks**, **Chef cookbooks** or **Puppet manifests** that Vagrant has built-in support for, as **provisioners**) are simply written in text files. This means that we can easily share the configurations and projects with colleagues, using version control systems such as Git.

When using Vagrant, the next time you need to go back to a previous project, you don't need to worry about any potential conflicts with changes made to your development environment (for example, if you have upgraded PHP, MySQL, or Apache on your local environment or within the Vagrant environment for another project), as the development environment for these projects are completely self-contained. If you bring a new member into the team, they can be up and running with your projects in minutes. Vagrant, along with its integration with provisioners, will take care of all the software and services needed to run the project on their machine. If you have one project that uses one web server such as Apache, and another one that uses Nginx, Vagrant lets you run these projects independently. If your project's production environment involves multiple servers (perhaps one for the Web and one for the database), Vagrant lets you emulate that with separate virtual servers on your machine.

With Vagrant:

- Your development environment can mimic the production environment
- Integrated provisioning tools such as Puppet, Chef, and Ansible allow you to store the configuration in a standard format, which can also be used to update production environments
- Each project is separate in its own virtualized environment, so issues as a result of configuration and version differences for dependencies on different projects are a thing of the past
- New team members can be onboarded to new projects as easy as `git clone && vagrant up`
- "It works on my machine" as a response to bugs is a thing of the past
- The headache of linking code that you write on your own machine to your virtualized development environment is taken care of through synced folders

- The environment can act as if it was your local machine and map the web server port (80) of your development machine to your development environment if you wish, or you can access it as you would another machine on your network
- You can let colleagues view your own development environment as well as easily share the development environment
- You can share access to your own development environment over the Internet to demo your project or to get support from a colleague
- Your local WAMP or MAMP installations will be gathering dust!

In this chapter, we will cover the following topics:

- Discuss the requirements and prerequisites for Vagrant
- Install Oracle VirtualBox
- Install Vagrant
- Verify that Vagrant was successfully installed

Once we have Vagrant and its prerequisites on our machine, we can then take a look at using it for our first project.

Requirements for Vagrant

Vagrant can be installed on Linux, Windows, and Mac OS X, and although it uses Ruby, the package includes an embedded Ruby interpreter. The only other requirement is a virtualization provider such as Oracle VirtualBox or VMware Fusion. The Oracle VirtualBox provider is available for free and is the default provider for Vagrant. So, we will use and install VirtualBox in order to use Vagrant during the course of this book. Other providers are available, including one for VMware Fusion or Workstation, which is available as a commercial add-on (http://www.vagrantup.com/vmware).

Getting started

Now that we know what software we need in order to get Vagrant running on our machine, let's start installing VirtualBox and Vagrant itself.

Installing VirtualBox

VirtualBox (https://www.virtualbox.org/) is an open source tool sponsored by Oracle that lets you create, manage, and use virtual machines on your own computer.

VirtualBox is a graphical program with a command-line interface that lets you visually create virtual machines, allocate resources, load external media such as operating system CDs, and view the screen of the virtual machine. Vagrant wraps on top of this and provides an intuitive command-line interface along with the integration of additional tools (including integrations with provisioners and also HashiCorp Atlas (formerly, Vagrant Cloud) that allow you to find and distribute base server images and share access to your Vagrant environments), so that we don't need to worry about how VirtualBox works or what to do with it; Vagrant takes care of this for us.

The first stage is to download the installer from the VirtualBox downloads page (https://www.virtualbox.org/wiki/Downloads), as shown in the following screenshot. We need to select the option that is appropriate for our computer (OS X, Windows, Linux, or Solaris):

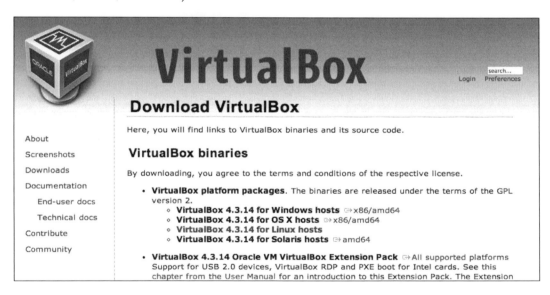

 At the time of writing this, Vagrant supports versions 4.0.x through 4.3.x of VirtualBox; earlier versions are not supported.

Once downloaded, let's open it and run the installer. On OS X, this involves clicking on the **VirtualBox.pkg** icon, as shown in the following screenshot. On Windows, simply opening the installer opens the installation wizard. On Linux, there are packages available that can be installed through your chosen package manager, see https://www.virtualbox.org/wiki/Linux_Downloads for more information.

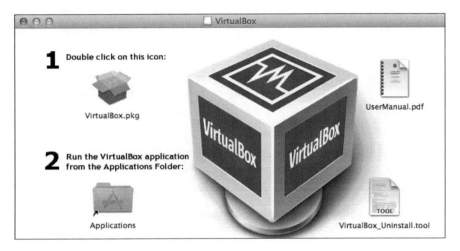

Before the installer runs, it first checks whether the computer is capable of having VirtualBox installed. We need to click on **Continue** to begin the installation process, as shown in the following screenshot. While this process will vary from OS X to Windows to Linux, the process is very similar across all platforms. There are fully detailed installation instructions for all platforms on the VirtualBox website (https://www.virtualbox.org/manual/ch02.html).

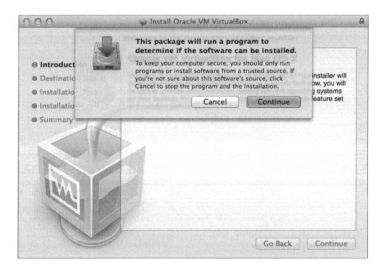

The first step in the process provides us with an introduction to the installation process and reminds us as to what we are actually installing:

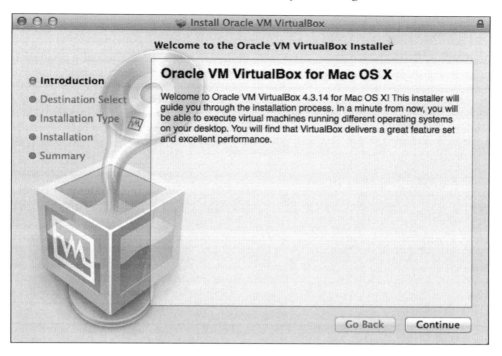

Next, the installer informs us as to how much space it will use on our computer, and provides us with the option to customize the installation if we want to **Change Install Location...**, and install the software in another location (perhaps another disk drive if our disk gets full).

Getting Started with Vagrant

Let's leave the default install location as it is, and click on the **Install** button to install VirtualBox on our computer:

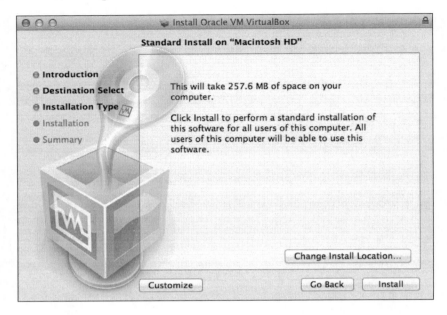

After being prompted to provide administrative privileges, the installer then automatically installs VirtualBox for us:

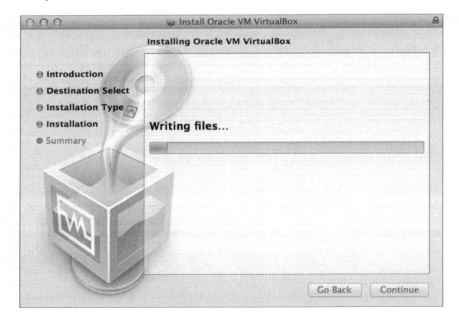

Once the installation has finished, we are shown a confirmation screen with the option of clicking on **Close** to close the installer:

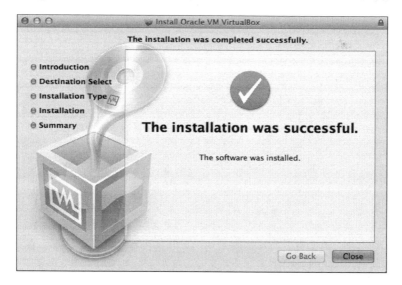

Now we have successfully installed VirtualBox!

Installing Vagrant

Now that we have the prerequisites installed on our computer, we can actually install Vagrant itself. This process is similar to that of installing VirtualBox. First, let's download the relevant installer from the Vagrant download page (http://www.vagrantup.com/downloads.html):

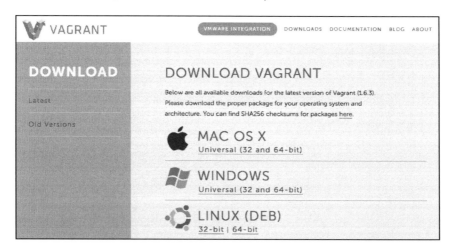

Let's open the installer and start the process. Again, on OS X, the first step is to double-click on the **Vagrant.pkg** icon:

We now need to follow the installation steps that are provided; this is very similar to the earlier steps for VirtualBox, and for most of the software packages in general. You might be prompted to provide your computer's administrative user privileges for the software to be installed.

Let's verify that Vagrant has been successfully installed. We can do this by opening a terminal window (cmd on Windows) and running the `vagrant` command:

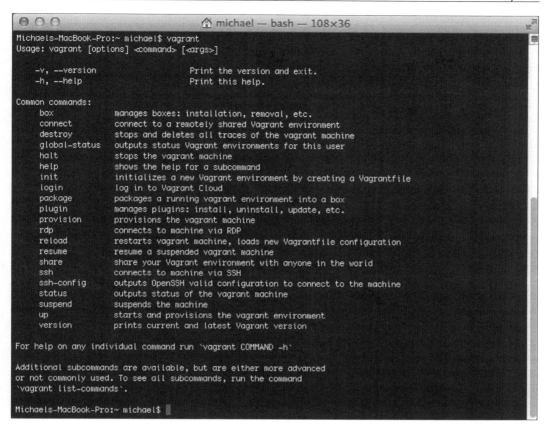

The preceding screenshot shows that we have successfully installed Vagrant, and we are able to run it.

Running the vagrant command on its own lists a range of common subcommands, which we can run within Vagrant, as well as instructions on how to access the help information on Vagrant and any of its subcommands. We can access the help information on Vagrant and its subcommands by adding the h flag, -h, to the end of the command when we run it.

Summary

In this chapter, we discussed the benefits of using virtualized development environments and specifically, Vagrant. We then installed Oracle VirtualBox, which is the virtualization provider Vagrant uses by default, and we installed Vagrant. After installing Vagrant, we ran the `vagrant` command to check whether it was installed correctly.

Now that we have Vagrant and a provider installed, we can now move onto using Vagrant to set up and manage some of our development projects in a virtual development environment. In the next chapter, we will create our first project, learn about the configuration file, and manage our Vagrant controlled machines.

2
Managing Vagrant Boxes and Projects

In this chapter, we will learn the basics of using Vagrant. We will take a look at initializing projects, importing base boxes to be used as our operating system, and controlling the virtual machine by powering on and off, suspending and resuming, and connecting to the box. Finally, we will also learn how to configure some of the key integration points between our own machine and our Vagrant-controlled virtual machine, including:

- Port forwarding
- Folder mapping
- Networking

Creating our first Vagrant project

Now that we have Vagrant installed on our machine, let's take a look at creating Vagrant projects. Any folder can act as a Vagrant project; it only requires a special configuration file, called the Vagrantfile, within it. Vagrant uses this file to set up the virtual machines (**guests**) and manage their integration with our computer (or **host** machine).

Vagrant has a command to create a Vagrantfile within the current directory you are in, within your computer's terminal: the `vagrant init` command. To create a new project, let's create a new folder anywhere in our system – ideally, somewhere easily reachable, then we need to go into this folder, and run the `init` command:

```
Michaels-iMac:Packt Reviews michael$ mkdir packt-vagrant-book
Michaels-iMac:Packt Reviews michael$ cd packt-vagrant-book/
Michaels-iMac:packt-vagrant-book michael$ vagrant init
```

Vagrant will then create a Vagrantfile within that folder, and show us a confirmation message:

```
Michaels-iMac:packt-vagrant-book michael$ vagrant init
A `Vagrantfile` has been placed in this directory. You are now
ready to `vagrant up` your first virtual environment! Please read
the comments in the Vagrantfile as well as documentation on
`vagrantup.com` for more information on using Vagrant.
Michaels-iMac:packt-vagrant-book michael$
```

If we take a look at the contents of this Vagrantfile file that was created, we will see a range of configuration options. Most of the options are commented out (as they are prefixed with a # character) to give us an idea of how we can configure the project.

There are only four lines of actual usable configuration in the file, as shown here:

```
VAGRANTFILE_API_VERSION = "2"
Vagrant.configure(VAGRANTFILE_API_VERSION) do |config|
  config.vm.box = "base"
end
```

> **Downloading the example code**
>
> You can download the example code files from your account at http://www.packtpub.com for all the Packt Publishing books you have purchased. If you purchased this book elsewhere, you can visit http://www.packtpub.com/support and register to have the files e-mailed directly to you.

Different versions of Vagrant use different structures and instructions within their Vagrantfile files. To make Vagrant backward compatible, the various settings are wrapped in a block of code that contains the version of the configuration to be used. Configuration Version 2 is compatible with Vagrant Version 1.1 up to Version 2.0.x (when released).

Within here, we have a single option — the type of Vagrant box to use. A Vagrant box is an image of an operating system that is configured to work with Vagrant.

We can generate a Vagrantfile without the illustrative comments by providing the minimal option (`-m` or `--minimal`, for example, `vagrant init --minimal`).

In order to boot our Vagrant machine, we run the `vagrant up` command:

```
Michaels-MacBook-Pro:packt-vagrant-book michael$ vagrant up
Bringing machine 'default' up with 'virtualbox' provider...
==> default: Box 'base' could not be found. Attempting to find and install...
    default: Box Provider: virtualbox
    default: Box Version: >= 0
==> default: Adding box 'base' (v0) for provider: virtualbox
    default: Downloading: base
An error occurred while downloading the remote file. The error
message, if any, is reproduced below. Please fix this error and try
again.

Couldn't open file /Users/michael/Documents/projects/packt-vagrant-book/base
Michaels-MacBook-Pro:packt-vagrant-book michael$
```

As Vagrant doesn't know what the box *base* is, our project is unable to boot. While Vagrant projects have their configuration stored *within* their projects folder, boxes are installed globally on your computer and can be shared across projects. If Vagrant doesn't have a box installed with that name, it will either try to download it from the URL provided in the Vagrantfile (if there is one provided) or it will look for the relevant box in HashiCorp Atlas (formerly Vagrant Cloud). HashiCorp, the company behind Vagrant, provides official boxes for the latest Long Term Support version of Ubuntu (this box is hosted on and distributed through Vagrant Cloud; we will discuss this in more detail in *Chapter 9, HashiCorp Atlas*). To use this box, we simply pass the name of the box to the `init` command (or update the Vagrantfile). As we already have a Vagrantfile in place for our project, we need to use the force option to override the existing file (`-f` or `--force`):

```
vagrant init --force hashicorp/precise64
```

Now if we try to run our Vagrant project, Vagrant will look for the box, and this time, it will download the `precise64` box from Vagrant Cloud, for use in our project:

```
Michaels-MacBook-Pro:packt-vagrant-book michael$ vagrant up
Bringing machine 'default' up with 'virtualbox' provider...
==> default: Box 'hashicorp/precise64' could not be found. Attempting to find and install...
    default: Box Provider: virtualbox
    default: Box Version: >= 0
==> default: Loading metadata for box 'hashicorp/precise64'
    default: URL: https://vagrantcloud.com/hashicorp/precise64
==> default: Adding box 'hashicorp/precise64' (v1.1.0) for provider: virtualbox
    default: Downloading: https://vagrantcloud.com/hashicorp/precise64/version/2/provider/virtualbox.box
    default: Progress: 1% (Rate: 257k/s, Estimated time remaining: 0:23:47)
```

Typically, boxes are minimal installations of operating systems that contain only what is required for the operating system to function, tools to integrate with Vagrant, and a minimal amount of other tools. This provides greater flexibility when it comes to using Vagrant to manage projects, as we can decide exactly what software we need to run on our virtual machine for our project to function, without having to worry about the conflicting versions of the said software. Some existing boxes may have more software installed, and of course, we may want to package a box that contains some of the key software our projects need (particularly, useful as a backup for users with unreliable Internet connections).

> While we are using commands to initialize our Vagrant projects in this chapter, these are simply quick ways to create a Vagrantfile file with some prepopulated values. A Vagrantfile file is the configuration file that defines how Vagrant should use the project (such as operating system to be used, virtual machines to boot up, synced folders, forwarded ports, and so on). We can, of course, create this file ourselves within the folder we wish to use as our project.

Managing Vagrant-controlled guest machines

The virtual machines, which Vagrant controls for us, still need to be managed and worked with. We have seen that we can start a Vagrant project with `vagrant up`. Let's learn more about this command, and see how to perform other operations on our new virtual machine.

Powering up a Vagrant-controlled virtual machine

As we have just seen, we can power up a virtual machine using the `vagrant up` command. With this command, Vagrant will first check whether a Vagrant environment has already been set up. If a previously suspended environment is found, it will resume that environment.

If the environment was not previously suspended, Vagrant then checks whether the base box has already been downloaded onto the machine. If it hasn't, it will download it, as it did for us when we booted our project with the `precise64` box for the first time.

Vagrant will then perform the following actions:

1. Copy the base box (remember, base boxes are managed globally on our host computer, so it takes a copy for each machine managed by it).
2. Create a new virtual machine with the relevant provider (the default being VirtualBox).
3. Forward any configured ports; by default, it will forward port 22 (the SSH port) on the virtual machine to port 2222 on the host. This will allow us to connect to the virtual machine over SSH.
4. Boot (power up) the virtual machine.
5. Configure and enable networking, so that we can communicate with the virtual machine.
6. Map shared folders between the host and the guest (by default, it will map the folder that contains the Vagrant project to `/vagrant` on the guest machine).
7. Run any provisioning tools that are set up such as Puppet, Chef, or SSH commands or scripts.

The actions performed by Vagrant will look something like this:

```
==> default: Importing base box 'hashicorp/precise64'...
==> default: Matching MAC address for NAT networking...
==> default: Checking if box 'hashicorp/precise64' is up to date...
==> default: Setting the name of the VM: packt-vagrant-book_default_1407708023282_51123
==> default: Fixed port collision for 22 => 2222. Now on port 2200.
==> default: Clearing any previously set network interfaces...
==> default: Preparing network interfaces based on configuration...
    default: Adapter 1: nat
==> default: Forwarding ports...
    default: 22 => 2200 (adapter 1)
==> default: Booting VM...
==> default: Waiting for machine to boot. This may take a few minutes...
    default: SSH address: 127.0.0.1:2200
    default: SSH username: vagrant
    default: SSH auth method: private key
    default: Warning: Connection timeout. Retrying...
==> default: Machine booted and ready!
==> default: Checking for guest additions in VM...
    default: The guest additions on this VM do not match the installed version of
    default: VirtualBox! In most cases this is fine, but in rare cases it can
    default: prevent things such as shared folders from working properly. If you see
    default: shared folder errors, please make sure the guest additions within the
    default: virtual machine match the version of VirtualBox you have installed on
    default: your host and reload your VM.
    default:
    default: Guest Additions Version: 4.2.0
    default: VirtualBox Version: 4.3
==> default: Mounting shared folders...
    default: /vagrant => /Users/michael/Documents/projects/packt-vagrant-book
Michaels-MacBook-Pro:packt-vagrant-book michael$
```

Suspending a virtual machine

We can save the current state of the virtual machine to the disk (suspend it) so that we can resume it later. If we run `vagrant suspend`, it will suspend the VM and stop it from consuming our machine's resources, except for the disk space it will occupy, ready for us to use again later:

```
Michaels-MacBook-Pro:packt-vagrant-book michael$ vagrant suspend
==> default: Saving VM state and suspending execution...
Michaels-MacBook-Pro:packt-vagrant-book michael$
```

Resuming a virtual machine

In order to use a previously suspended virtual machine, we simply run `vagrant resume`:

```
Michaels-MacBook-Pro:packt-vagrant-book michael$ vagrant resume
==> default: Resuming suspended VM...
==> default: Booting VM...
==> default: Waiting for machine to boot. This may take a few minutes...
    default: SSH address: 127.0.0.1:2200
    default: SSH username: vagrant
    default: SSH auth method: private key
    default: Warning: Connection refused. Retrying...
==> default: Machine booted and ready!
Michaels-MacBook-Pro:packt-vagrant-book michael$
```

Shutting down a virtual machine

We can shut down a running virtual machine using the `vagrant halt` command. This instructs the VM to stop all running processes and shut down. To use it again, we need to run `vagrant up`, which will power on the machine; provisioning is typically only ran on the first `vagrant up` command. To ensure that provisioning runs when we boot up a saved machine subsequently, we can use the `--provision` flag.

```
Michaels-MacBook-Pro:packt-vagrant-book michael$ vagrant halt
==> default: Attempting graceful shutdown of VM...
Michaels-MacBook-Pro:packt-vagrant-book michael$
```

Starting from scratch

Sometimes, things go wrong. It's not inconceivable that we might make some changes to our virtual machine, and find out that it no longer works. Thankfully, since we have a base box, configuration file, and provisioning files, which are all stored separately, we can instruct Vagrant to destroy our virtual machine, and then create it again, using the configurations to set it up. This is done via the `destroy` command, and then we need to use the `up` command to start it again:

```
vagrant destroy
vagrant up
```

Of course, if we update our Vagrantfile, provisioning manifests, or application code that can also break things; so it is important that we use a version control system to properly manage our project's code and configuration, so that we can undo the changes there too; Vagrant can only do so much to help us!

Updating based on Vagrantfile changes

If we make changes to our Vagrantfile, these changes won't apply until we next shut down and power on our virtual machine. As this isn't very convenient, there is a handy `reload` command that will shut down the machine, reload its configuration based on the Vagrantfile as it currently is, and boot it up again:

`vagrant reload`

Running this command yields the following result:

```
Michaels-MacBook-Pro:packt-vagrant-book michael$ vagrant reload
==> default: Attempting graceful shutdown of VM...
==> default: Checking if box 'hashicorp/precise64' is up to date...
==> default: Clearing any previously set forwarded ports...
==> default: Fixed port collision for 22 => 2222. Now on port 2200.
==> default: Clearing any previously set network interfaces...
==> default: Preparing network interfaces based on configuration...
    default: Adapter 1: nat
==> default: Forwarding ports...
    default: 22 => 2200 (adapter 1)
==> default: Booting VM...
==> default: Waiting for machine to boot. This may take a few minutes...
    default: SSH address: 127.0.0.1:2200
    default: SSH username: vagrant
    default: SSH auth method: private key
    default: Warning: Connection timeout. Retrying...
==> default: Machine booted and ready!
==> default: Checking for guest additions in VM...
    default: The guest additions on this VM do not match the installed version of
    default: VirtualBox! In most cases this is fine, but in rare cases it can
    default: prevent things such as shared folders from working properly. If you see
    default: shared folder errors, please make sure the guest additions within the
    default: virtual machine match the version of VirtualBox you have installed on
    default: your host and reload your VM.
    default:
    default: Guest Additions Version: 4.2.0
    default: VirtualBox Version: 4.3
==> default: Mounting shared folders...
    default: /vagrant => /Users/michael/Documents/projects/packt-vagrant-book
==> default: Machine already provisioned. Run `vagrant provision` or use the `--provision`
==> default: to force provisioning. Provisioners marked to run always will still run.
Michaels-MacBook-Pro:packt-vagrant-book michael$
```

Connecting to the virtual machine over SSH

If we run the `vagrant ssh` command, Vagrant will then connect to the virtual machine over SSH. Alternatively, we can SSH to localhost with port `2222`, and this will tunnel into the virtual machine, using the default forwarded SSH port.

If we run Vagrant on a Windows machine, we won't have a built-in SSH client. We can use a client such as **PuTTY** to connect to Vagrant. PuTTY can be downloaded from `http://www.chiark.greenend.org.uk/~sgtatham/putty/`. More information on how to configure PuTTY to work with Vagrant is available on the Vagrant website (`http://docs-v1.vagrantup.com/v1/docs/getting-started/ssh.html`).

Managing integration between host and guest machines

Without any form of integration between the host machine and the guest, we would simply have a bare bones virtual server running on top of our own operating system, which is not particularly useful. We need our own machine to be capable of integrating tightly with the guest (virtual machine).

Port forwarding

Although the virtual machine is running on our own machine, because of virtualization, it acts and behaves like a completely different machine. Sometimes, this is what we want; however, there might be times we want to have the virtual machine behave almost as an extension of our own machine. One way to do this is through **port forwarding**, where we can tunnel a port from the virtual machine to a port on the host machine. If, for example, we have a web server running on our own machine, we obviously don't want to map the web server port from Vagrant onto the same port; otherwise, there would be a conflict. Instead, we can map it to another port. If we map the web server port on the virtual machine to port `8888` on the host, then navigating to `http://localhost:8888` on our own machine would show us the web service we run on the guest, despite the fact that the localhost refers to our host machine.

The port forwarding is done via lines in the `Vagrantfile` file; we simply provide the guest and host ports we wish to map:

```
config.vm.network :forwarded_port, guest: 80, host: 8888
```

If we have other Vagrant managed virtual machines on our computer, which we wish to run simultaneously, we can enable `auto_correct` on specific ports. This way, if a conflict is found (for example, two virtual machines trying to map to the same port), one virtual machine will try a different port instead:

```
, auto_correct: true
```

Ports below a certain range need elevated or root privileges on the host machine, so you may be asked for your administrative password.

Synced folders

Synced folders allow us to share a folder between the host and the guest. By default, Vagrant shares the folder that contains the Vagrant project `/vagrant` on the virtual machine. We can use the following command in our `Vagrantfile` to sync more folders if we wish:

```
config.vm.synced_folder "/Users/michael/assets/" "/var/www/assets"
```

The first parameter is the path to the folder on our machine and the second is the mount point on the VM. If we use a relative path on our machine, it would be relative to the project folder.

If we want to override the default synced folder, we can do this too:

```
    config.vm.synced_folder ".", "/var/another/folder"
```

The **Network File System** (**NFS**) can give us better performance with synced folders than the default settings. This won't have any effect on Windows hosts, and on Linux/OS X, hosts will require root privileges. We can enable NFS on a per synced folder basis by adding the following command to the preceding line:

```
    , type: "nfs"
```

Networking

By default, our Vagrant virtual machines are only accessible from the machines we run Vagrant on, and other machines in our network won't be able to access them. If we map ports to our host, then we can share the services running on the virtual machine with our colleagues within our network. If we want to allow our colleagues to access our Vagrant managed virtual machines directly, we can attach the virtual machine to our internal network, and VirtualBox will bridge the network between our machine and the virtual machine, and the internal network between our machine and the rest of the machines in our home or office.

```
    config.vm.network "private_network", ip: "10.11.100.200"
```

This approach is also useful when wanting to have multiple Vagrant projects running at the same time; if they are web projects, they can all expose port 80, but on different IP addresses, and if we want, we can map these to the hostnames in our hosts file.

>
> The hosts file is a file on a computer that maps a domain name to an IP address. This can be used to prevent the computer from having to look up the IP address for a domain and is useful for locally hosted sites, as we can manually link the IP address to a domain name, just for our local machine. On OS X and Linux, the hosts file is stored as /etc/hosts, and on Windows it is stored as C:\Windows\System32\Drivers\etc\hosts.
>
> If we want to share access to our virtual machine or demo something running on it, we can use Vagrant Share through Vagrant Cloud, which we will discuss in *Chapter 9*, *HashiCorp Atlas*.

It is also possible to have the IP address assigned via DHCP (typically, this will mean that your network's router will assign it an IP address):

```
config.vm.network "private_network", type: "dhcp"
```

Autorunning commands

One of the key concepts within Vagrant is **provisioning**. This involves turning a basic virtual machine with a base operating system into a server that is ready to run for your project, meeting your requirements. To go from the base operating system to a fully fledged machine, we need to use a provisioning tool to install the software and configure the machine. There are a number of key provisioning options within Vagrant:

- Shell
- Puppet
- Ansible
- Chef

Puppet, Ansible, and Chef are all third-party tools that Vagrant supports out of the box, and provide specific languages to configure servers in an agnostic way that can be used for different operating systems. The next three chapters will discuss these tools in more detail. Vagrant also supports some other provisioning tools, including **Salt**, **Docker**, and **CFEngine**.

SSH provisioning involves running a series of commands on the virtual machine over SSH when the machine is first set up.

There are two key ways in which we can use SSH provisioning. We can either directly run a command from our `Vagrantfile` or we can run the contents of a script.

The following line in our `Vagrantfile` will run the inline command provided:

```
config.vm.provision "shell", inline: "sudo apt-get update"
```

Alternatively, we can tell Vagrant to run a particular shell script (the location of the script specified is relative to our project root, that is, `/vagrant`):

```
config.vm.provision "shell", path: "provision.sh"
```

This shell script could contain all of the commands we need to convert a base box into a box, which supports our project and application, perhaps installing web and database servers.

Managing Vagrant boxes

We can manage Vagrant boxes using the `vagrant box` command. Let's run this command with the help flag (`--help`) and see what subcommands are available:

```
vagrant box --help
```

Running this command gives the following result:

```
Michaels-MacBook-Pro:packt-vagrant-book michael$ vagrant box --help
Usage: vagrant box <subcommand> [<args>]

Available subcommands:
     add
     list
     outdated
     remove
     repackage
     update

For help on any individual subcommand run `vagrant box <subcommand> -h`

Michaels-MacBook-Pro:packt-vagrant-book michael$
```

There are six available box-related subcommands. With each of these, we can provide the `--help` flag to see what additional arguments are available. The available box-related subcommands are:

- `add`: This command adds a new box
- `list`: This command lists all boxes installed
- `outdated`: This command checks whether any boxes have updates available
- `remove`: This command removes a box from the host
- `repackage`: This command converts a Vagrant environment into a distributable box
- `update`: This command will update the box being used by the current running Vagrant environment

Adding Vagrant boxes

The `add` subcommand allows us to add a new box. It takes a single argument and a number of optional flags. The argument is a name, URL, or path to a box file. If a name is provided, Vagrant will download the box from Vagrant Cloud. If we provide a URL or path to a box stored elsewhere, we need to give Vagrant a name to use. This is provided with the `--name` optional flag.

Some other optional flags that might be useful include: `--force`, which will tell Vagrant to remove a pre-existing box with the same name; `--clean`, which will tell Vagrant to clean any temporary downloaded files; and `--provider`, which allows us to specify another provider to back the box (the default provider being VirtualBox, however, there are providers available for Vagrant, including VMware and Amazon EC2).

The following command will add a new `packt` box, and if an existing one is found, it will override it:

```
vagrant box add --force packt http://our-server.vagrant/packt.box
```

The process of adding a box may take a while, as most Vagrant boxes will be at least 200 MB big. Once downloaded, the box will be extracted and available for us to use in our Vagrant projects, as we observed when we started our first project earlier in the chapter.

Listing Vagrant boxes

The `list` subcommand will list the boxes installed within Vagrant, along with the provider that backs the box:

vagrant box list

Running this command gives the following output:

```
Michaels-MacBook-Pro:packt-vagrant-book michael$ vagrant box list
hashicorp/precise64 (virtualbox, 1.1.0)
precise64           (virtualbox, 0)
quantal64           (virtualbox, 0)
quantal64_roderik   (virtualbox, 0)
ubuntu/trusty64     (virtualbox, 14.04)
Michaels-MacBook-Pro:packt-vagrant-book michael$
```

Checking for updates

Boxes, which are provided by Vagrant Cloud, may be regularly updated; we can use the `outdated` subcommand to see whether there are updates available:

```
Michaels-MacBook-Pro:packt-vagrant-book michael$ vagrant box outdated
Checking if box 'hashicorp/precise64' is up to date...
Michaels-MacBook-Pro:packt-vagrant-book michael$
```

Removing Vagrant boxes

We can remove the box with the `remove` subcommand. We need to provide the name of the box to be removed. Optionally, we can also specify the provider and the version of the box to be removed with the `--provider` and `--box-version` flags, respectively. The following example will remove our `precise64` box for VirtualBox:

vagrant box remove hashicorp/precise64 --provider virtualbox

Running this command gives the following output:

```
Michaels-MacBook-Pro:packt-vagrant-book michael$ vagrant box remove hashicorp/precise64 --provider virtualbox
Removing box 'hashicorp/precise64' (v1.1.0) with provider 'virtualbox'...
Michaels-MacBook-Pro:packt-vagrant-book michael$
```

Repackaging a Vagrant box

The `repackage` subcommand lets us convert a Vagrant environment complete with any customizations we have made to it, such as software we have installed on it, into a box that we can reuse and distribute to others. We will use this command in *Chapter 8, Creating Your Own Box*.

Updating the current environment's box

We can use the `update` subcommand to update the box in use on the current Vagrant environment:

```
vagrant box update
```

Alternatively, we can update a specific box, which isn't tied to the current environment, using the `--box` flag to provide the name of the box (and the `--provider` option too if we wish).

Too many Vagrants!

Once we start using Vagrant on a range of projects, the lack of a GUI can make it easy to lose track of which projects are running or suspended on your machine. This is especially annoying when you want to boot up a new project, but an existing Vagrant project is either causing a conflict or consuming too many resources on your machine. Thankfully, there is now a command to list all active Vagrant environments on your host, for example,

This command lists the IDs, names, providers, and states of our Vagrant projects as well as the directory they are running in:

```
id       name     provider    state    directory
---------------------------------------------------------------
77e5115  default  virtualbox  saved    /Users/michael/projects/l
94a3b13  default  virtualbox  saved    /Users/michael/projects/a
7bed41c  default  virtualbox  saved    /Users/michael/projects/l
ef7178d  default  virtualbox  running  /Users/michael/projects/v
dbee537  default  virtualbox  saved    /Users/michael/projects/p
6e84e25  default  virtualbox  saved    /Users/michael/projects/u
169cb08  default  virtualbox  saved    /Users/michael/projects/s
60e22d3  default  virtualbox  running  /Users/michael/projects/s
```

We can append the ID to the end of the `vagrant` command to run the command against that machine, without having to go into that folder, for example:

`vagrant suspend 77e5115`

Summary

In this chapter, we created projects with Vagrant, imported a base box to use, and booted our Vagrant environment. We also looked at the commands needed to manage these boxes and the Vagrant virtual machines. We looked at how we can configure our Vagrant environment with networking, synced folders, and forwarded ports, and how to provision software on our virtual machine with SSH commands. When it becomes a problem to have multiple Vagrant projects running, we now know how to locate these running projects with the `global-status` command.

In the next chapter, we will take a look at how to use Puppet, one of the provisioning tools supported by Vagrant. We will cover installing and configuring services, managing files and folders, running commands, and managing users and scheduled tasks.

3
Provisioning with Puppet

Vagrant is a very powerful tool primarily because of the following key concepts it can manage for us:

- Virtualization
- Provisioning
- Box distribution
- Sharing

In *Chapter 1, Getting Started with Vagrant* and *Chapter 2, Managing Vagrant Boxes and Projects*, we learned to use Vagrant to manage virtual machines for us. While this is useful, at this stage, these virtual machines are dumb; they have very little software installed for us to use, and they are certainly not configured for our projects.

There are two approaches we can use to set up a Vagrant-managed virtual machine with all the software required for a project:

- Use a base box that is preconfigured with the software or development stack that we require
- Provision the exact software and configuration that we require using a provisioning tool

Preconfigured base boxes are useful and have their place. If we were always using a specific configuration or we were creating a Vagrant environment for an open source project we were releasing, a configured box might be the best option. In that instance, a configured base box will quickly get users up and running on the project. The downside is that it isn't easy to change the configuration as the needs of the project change, and certain elements such as cron jobs and background workers would still need to be configured separately.

Provisioning, however, automates the process of turning a base machine into one that is configured for use with a specific project.

In this chapter, we will quickly take a look at the basics of Puppet, one of the various provisioning options available within Vagrant. We won't look at it within a Vagrant context just yet; we will simply take a look at how a Puppet works, and how we can use it. In *Chapter 6, Provisioning Vagrant Machines with Puppet, Ansible, and Chef*, we will take a look at how to connect what we will learn in this chapter with Vagrant itself. In this chapter, we will learn the following topics:

- How Puppet works
- The basics behind Puppet modules and manifests
- How to use Puppet to perform the following tasks:
    - Install software
    - Manage files and folders within the filesystem
    - Manage cron jobs
    - Run commands
    - Manage users and groups
- Creating configurable classes
- How to use third-party Puppet modules and Puppet Forge
- How to manually run Puppet to provision a machine

Puppet itself is a large topic and the subject of several books. For a more detailed look at Puppet, Packt Publishing has some titles dedicated to it:

- *Puppet 2.7 Cookbook, John Arundel* (`http://www.packtpub.com/puppet-2-7-for-reliable-secure-systems-cloud-computing-cookbook/book`)
- *Puppet 3: Beginners Guide, John Arundel* (`http://www.packtpub.com/puppet-3-beginners-guide/book`)

Provisioning

Within this context, provisioning is the process of setting up a virtual machine so that it can be used for a specific purpose or project. Typically, this involves installing software, configuring the software, managing services running on the machine, and even setting up users and groups on the machine.

For a web-based software project, provisioning will likely entail the installation of a web server, a programming language, and a database system. Configuration changes will be needed to set up a database on the database system and to allow the web server to write to specific folders (to deal with user uploads).

Without this provisioning process, we would have an almost vanilla install of an operating system, which contains a synced copy of our project folder; this vanilla install wouldn't be usable as a development environment for our project. Provisioning takes us to the next level and gives us a fully working environment for our project.

Puppet

Puppet is a provisioning tool that we can use to set up a server for use for a project. The configuration that determines how the server needs to be set up can be stored within our Vagrant project and can be shared with teammates through a version control, ensuring everyone gets an up-to-date copy of the required development environment.

Information about how a server should be configured, that is, its software, files, users, and groups, is written into files known as the Puppet manifests. These manifests are written using Puppet's own language, which is a Ruby domain-specific language. Puppet takes this information and compiles it into a catalog that is specific for the operating system it is being applied to. The catalog is then applied to the machine.

For our purposes, we will use Puppet in standalone mode (this is also how Vagrant uses it). Standalone mode means that everything runs from one machine. Puppet also has client-server capabilities, where you can define the Puppet manifests for all the servers in your infrastructure, on a central host, and it keeps your individual servers at the required level of configuration.

Puppet is **idempotent**, which means running Puppet on a machine multiple times has the same effect as running it only once. In effect, Puppet ensures that conditions are met, and if they are not, it will perform actions to ensure that they are met, for example, Puppet would install Nginx if it wasn't already installed. If it was already installed, it would do nothing. This means we can reprovision with Puppet many times without any detrimental effect. This is useful as we can use it to keep the server in sync with our Puppet manifests if they were to change.

Creating modules and manifests with Puppet

Puppet is made up of a manifest file and a number of modules (which also contain manifests and other resources). The default manifest specifies which modules are to be used, and depending on the module, provides customization options for it (for example, the Puppet module for **supervisord** (http://supervisord.org/), a process control system, allows us to specify any number of processes that should be managed using supervisord through the module itself).

Modules make use of resources within Puppet to control and configure the machine, and these modules can be imported to run in a specific sequence, through stages.

Puppet classes

Puppet modules typically consist of classes, which, in turn, utilize a number of resource types (in this example, the `package` resource type, to install a software package) to achieve a specific requirement for our server. It effectively allows us to bundle a number of these resource types in a way, which means we can simply include the class by its name, and have all of the instructions executed from within it.

A class in its most basic form is structured as follows:

```
class nginx {
  package { "nginx":
    ensure => present,
    require => Exec['apt-get update']
  }
}
```

For its most basic use within Vagrant, classes such as these will be saved as `default.pp` within the `modules/nginx/manifests/` folder. The class can contain many resource types to achieve a desired goal (for instance, installing the Apache package isn't the same as preparing the web server fully for a project, related tasks can be bundled into the same class).

Default Puppet manifests

For a given project, Puppet modules are typically all located in a specific `modules` directory. Many modules can be customized when they are run, an example being the `supervisord` module; it simply provides the structure for us to customize for each process we want it to manage.

Because of this, we need to have a default Puppet manifest that includes a list of modules to be run and any configurations for them. Because Puppet is aware of our module folder location when we run it (and when it is run through Vagrant), we just list the modules to be included and run.

A basic manifest that will include and run the `nginx` class we wrote earlier would be as follows:

```
import "nginx"
include nginx
```

I mentioned the `supervisor` module (https://github.com/plathrop/puppet-module-supervisor) a few times as a module that is designed to be used for multiple different things, which can be customized by the developer using it.

> Supervisord is the name of the software, however, the Puppet module we are going to use to manage supervisord is called supervisor (no "d")—so watch out for that!

Supervisord is a tool that maintains a number of running processes, for example, if you have a background worker in a web application to resize images, the supervisor might be responsible for keeping five workers running at any one instance, respawning them when one has finished. The following is an example of how this module would be used in a default Puppet manifest:

```
supervisor::service {
  'resize_images':
    ensure      => present,
    command     => '/usr/bin/php /vagrant/app/console img:resize',
    user        => 'root',
    group       => 'root',
    autorestart => true,
    startsecs   => 0,
    num_procs   => 5,
    require     => [ Package['php5-cli'], Package['beanstalkd'] ];
}

supervisor::service {
  email':
    ensure      => present,
    command     => '/usr/bin/php /vagrant/app/console email',
    user        => 'root',
```

```
            group        => 'root',
            autorestart  => true,
            startsecs    => 0,
            num_procs    => 5,
            require      => [ Package['php5-cli'], Package['beanstalkd'] ];
    }
```

Here, we are instructing Puppet to use the supervisord module twice to set up and manage two workers for us. For each of the workers, we have a set of five processes to be run, and we have set the user and group to run them. We have defined PHP's command-line interface and the `beanstalkd` worker queue as requirements for the workers. This illustrates the power that Puppet modules have.

Resources

Puppet provides a range of resource types that we can utilize to create our configuration files. These resource types are translated and compiled depending on the operating system being used. For example, if we were to use the `package` resource type to install some software, this would use `apt-get` on Ubuntu and `Yum` on Fedora operating systems. A small number of resource types are operating system specific, for example the `scheduled_task` resource type is designed specifically for Windows, and the `cron` type is designed for Linux and Unix-based systems.

Resource types available include:

- **Cron**: This resource type is used to manage cron jobs on Linux- and Unix-based systems
- **Exec**: This resource type is used to run commands at the terminal/command prompt
- **File**: This resource type is used to manage and manipulate files and folders on the filesystem
- **Group**: This resource type is used to manage user groups
- **Package**: This resource type is used to install software
- **Service**: This resource type is used to manage running services on the machine
- **User**: This resource type is used to manage user accounts on the machine

When resource types are used directly (for example, we use the `Package` resource type to install some software), they are used in lowercase (`package`). However, when we refer to a resource type we have used, for example, as a requirement for another Puppet action, we reference them with a leading capital letter (`Package`).

An example of this is as follows:

```
package { "nginx":
   ensure => present,
   require => Exec['apt-get update']
}
```

We tell Puppet to install the `nginx` package (lowercase "p" for `package`), but when we specify the requirement of a previously executed `exec` command, we use a leading capital letter. The options within this instruction for Puppet (`ensure` and `require` keywords) are called **parameters**.

A full list of resource types is available on the Puppet website at `http://docs.puppetlabs.com/references/latest/type.html`.

When using a resource type, a name is provided (in the preceding instance, this is `nginx`), this is often dual purpose, serving both as a way for us to reference the action (in this case, the package being installed) and also as an instruction (in this case, what package Puppet needs to install). When it comes to the `Exec` resource type, the name is the command we wish to run. By default, we need to provide the full path to the command that we run. We can avoid this by providing the path from which the command should be run as a parameter.

Resource requirements

Certain things that we do with Puppet will require other actions to have been performed first. These can be defined using the `require` parameter, and we can specify multiple requirements.

If we need to run or install something after both the MySQL Server and the MySQL client packages have been installed, we will use the `require` parameter to define them as follows:

```
require => [ Package['mysql-client'], Package['mysql-server'] ]
```

This defines an array of multiple requirements as a dependency for our Puppet code.

Resource execution ordering

Sometimes, we need to run specific blocks of the Puppet code before other blocks. In most cases, we can use the `require`, `notify`, and `subscribe` parameters to get around this problem.

The notify, subscribe, and refreshonly parameters

Sometimes, we want to have a Puppet command run multiple times when other commands have finished. One example is to restart the `nginx` service. We will perform the following steps:

1. Import a new configuration file.
2. Add new virtual hosts.

We can use the `notify` parameter to instruct one command to trigger another to be run. In effect, this notifies the next command to tell it that there have been changes made elsewhere, which requires that command to now run.

In the following example, we require a Puppet managed configuration file to be copied to our Puppet managed machine. The code requires Nginx to be installed before it is run, and after the file has been copied across, it will notify the `nginx` service to be restarted. Importantly, this notification will be run each time the file changes, but won't be triggered when it runs where the file is unchanged:

```
file { '/etc/nginx/sites-available/default':
    source => "puppet:///modules/nginx/default",
    owner => 'root',
    group => 'root',
    notify => Service['nginx'],
    require => Package['nginx']
}
```

This can be also be achieved using the `subscribe` and `refreshonly` parameters, which work in the opposite way to `notify`. The `subscribe` parameter instructs the command to run every time any of the commands in the `subscribe` option have been run.

The `refreshonly` parameter, when set to `true`, instructs the command to only run when one of the commands it subscribes to has run (leaving this out would mean the command is also run in its own right):

```
service { "nginx":
    refreshonly => false,
    subscribe => File['/etc/nginx/sites-available/default'],
}
```

Here, the command to reload Nginx will only be run when the new configuration file has been loaded. We can, of course, extend the `subscribe` parameter to contain other things such as modules and other configurations, as discussed earlier.

Chapter 3

 Only `service`, `exec`, and `mount` resource types can be refreshed.

Executing resources in stages

Where `require`, `notify`, and `subscribe` are not suitable for our use case, we can use **stages**. Puppet has a default stage, within which all commands run. We can create our own stages, which run before or after this stage that allow us to force commands to be run in specific orders.

We can define stages within our default Puppet manifest and then instruct Puppet to run certain classes from within that stage. If, for example, we wanted to run our `Nginx` class before anything else, we can create a stage to run first, and put the `Nginx` class within that stage as follows:

```
stage { 'first': before => Stage[main] }
class {'nginx': stage => first}
```

This creates a stage called `first`, and anything assigned to this stage will be executed before the default Puppet stage; next, it places the `Nginx` class within that stage. Once we have a named stage, such as `first`, we can then create other stages, which can run before this one too.

 Stages are useful when you need to group the ordering of certain tasks, however, they can normally be avoided through the proper use of `require`, `notify`, and `subscribe`, which should be used instead where possible.

Installing software

Let's say we want to install Nginx on our server. There are three typical steps involved in this process:

1. Updating our package manager.
2. Installing the `nginx` package.
3. Running the `nginx` service.

Because the first step is different, depending on the operating system we are running, we would want to either move this out of Puppet at a later stage or look at using a module to abstract it out, however, we will use it within Puppet for the time being. Any operating specific commands (such as these) are written for Ubuntu, which is the operating system we are using with Vagrant. If you are not using Ubuntu, the `Exec` command should be rewritten to update the package manager on your system.

Provisioning with Puppet

 This example is purely to illustrate the process of putting together a simple module. There are many existing modules available on Puppet Forge, which we will come to later.

Updating our package manager

In order to update our package manager, we need to run a command on the server. This can be achieved using the `Exec` resource within Puppet:

```
exec { 'apt-get update':
    command => '/usr/bin/apt-get update',
    timeout => 0
}
```

This instructs Puppet to run the `apt-get update` command. We have set a timeout of zero so that if it takes a while (and after a fresh installation of an operating system through Vagrant, it might), Puppet will run it for as long as it takes, overriding the default timeout.

 This isn't the most elegant of approaches, especially with it being operating system specific and subsequently a requirement for most of our other commands. In *Appendix, A Sample LEMP Stack*, we will build a **LEMP** server project with Vagrant and Puppet, and in the example, we use Vagrant's SSH provisioning options to update the package manager before we install the other software. Most base boxes don't have up-to-date package details to save space and due to their age, so updating the package manager is required.

Installing the nginx package

We can use the `Package` resource to ensure that Nginx is installed, and if it isn't, it will be installed as follows:

```
package { "nginx":
   ensure => present,
      require => Exec['apt-get update']
}
```

Here, we told Puppet to ensure that the `nginx` package is present. We added our `apt-get update` command as a prerequisite, so we know that our packages will be up to date.

[44]

Running the nginx service

Finally, to make sure that Nginx is running, we use the `Service` resource to ensure that the `nginx` service is running. Obviously, this can't be run if Nginx isn't installed, so the `nginx` package is a prerequisite:

```
service { "nginx":
    ensure => running,
      require => Package['nginx']
}
```

File management

We can use the `File` resource within Puppet to manage files and folders within the filesystem. Let's take a look at some examples, which allow us to:

- Copy files
- Create symlinks
- Create folders
- Create multiple folders in one go

Copying a file

One common file operation we might want to perform would be to take a configuration file from our project and copy it into our virtual machine. One particular use case would be an Nginx configuration file; we might want to define some virtual hosts and other settings in a file, which we can share with our colleagues.

> While this works well and can get us up and running quickly, there are modules out there that allow us to configure Nginx and other types of software directly from Puppet. This typically works by the module of storing a template file (a copy of the configuration file with placeholders in it) and then, inserting data that we define within Puppet into the template, and copying the file onto the machine. However, for the sake of this introductory chapter, we will just copy a file across.

Provisioning with Puppet

The `file` resource type allows us to create files, folders, and symlinks. In order to create a file (or replace the contents of an existing file with another file), we simply tell Puppet what file we want to create or replace (the destination), the source (that is, the file to be copied and put into the destination), and the user and group who should own the file:

```
file { '/etc/nginx/sites-available/default':
  source => 'puppet://modules/nginx/default',
  owner  => 'root',
  group  => 'root',
  require => Package['nginx']
}
```

As this is an Nginx configuration file, it is worth ensuring that Nginx is already installed; otherwise, Nginx will override this when it installs the first time and this wouldn't make the process idempotent.

> Here's something to note about file locations: the source file in the preceding file resource code is held within a Vagrant environment and the Puppet module itself. We can provide two kinds of file paths: either the full path to the file on the machine, which Puppet is running on (our Vagrant environment), such as `/vagrant/path/to/default` or a path relative to Puppet modules. These Puppet paths are structured like this: `puppet:///modules/nginx/default`. The difference you will note is that it automatically looks for in the files/ folder within the `nginx` folder; we don't need to specify that.

Creating a symlink

If we omit the `source` parameter and instead add an `ensure` parameter, and set that to `link`, we can create a **symlink**. A target is used to define where the symlink should point to, as shown in the following code:

```
file { '/var/www/vendor':
  ensure => 'link',
    target => '/vagrant/vendor',
      require => Package['nginx']
}
```

Creating folders

Similar to the preceding symlink code, this time, we simply need to set `ensure` to a directory. This will then create a directory for us as follows:

```
file{ "/var/www/uploads":
    ensure => "directory",
    owner  => "www-data",
    group  => "www-data"
    mode   => 777,
}
```

We can use the `mode` parameter to set the permissions of the folder (this also can be used for files we create and manage).

Creating multiple folders in one go

In many web projects, we might need to create a number of folders within our servers or our Vagrant virtual machines. In particular, we might want to create a number of `cache` folders for different parts of our application, or we might want to create some `upload` folders.

In order to do this, we can simply create an array that contains all of the folders we want to create. We can then use the `file` resource type and pass the array to create them all, as follows:

```
$cache_directories = [
   "/var/www/cache/",
   "/var/www/cache/pages",
   "/var/www/cache/routes",
   "/var/www/cache/templates",
]

file { $cache_directories:
    ensure => "directory",
    owner  => "www-data",
    group  => "www-data",
    mode   => 777,
}
```

Cron management

The `cron` resource type lets us use Puppet to manage cron jobs, which we need to run on the machine. We provide a name, in this case, `web_cron`, the command to run, the user to run the command as, and the times at which to run the command, as shown in the following code:

```
cron { web_cron:
    command => "/usr/bin/php /vagrant/cron.php",
    user    => "root",
    hour    => [1-4],
    minute  => [0,30],
}
```

Puppet provides us with different configuration options to define the times at which a cron should be run, which includes the following:

- **Hour**: This value is between 0 and 23 inclusive
- **Minute**: This value is between 0 and 59 inclusive
- **Month**: This value is between 1 and 12 inclusive
- **MonthDay**: This value is between 1 and 31 inclusive
- **Weekday**: This value is Sunday (7 or 0) to Saturday (6)

If one of these is omitted from the configuration, then Puppet runs it for each one of the available options (that is, if we omit month, it will run for January through to December). When defining the dates and times, we can either provide a range, for example, [1-5] or specifics, such as [1, 2, 10, 12].

Running commands

The `Exec` resource type allows us to run commands through the terminal on the machine we are provisioning. One caveat with the `exec` command is that if you reprovision with Puppet, it will rerun the command, which can be damaging depending on the command. What we can do with the `Exec` resource type is set the `creates` parameter. The `creates` parameter tells Puppet that a file will be created when the command is run, and if Puppet finds that file, it knows that it has already been run and won't run it again.

Take for example, the following configuration; this will use the PHP composer tool to download dependencies. The command itself creates a file called `composer.lock` (we can, of course, use the `exec` command itself to create a file manually, perhaps using the `touch` command). Because of the lock file that is created, we can use the `creates` parameter to prevent the command from being executed if it has previously been executed and has created the lock file, as shown in the following code:

```
exec{ "compose":
    command => '/bin/rm -rfv /var/www/repo/vendor/* && /bin/rm -f
     /var/www/repo/composer.lock && /usr/bin/curl -s
       http://getcomposer.org/installer | /usr/bin/php && cd
         /var/www/repo && /usr/bin/php /var/www/repo/composer.
           phar install',
    require => [ Package['curl'], Package['git-core'] ],
    creates => "/var/www/repo/composer.lock",
    timeout => 0
}
```

Managing users and groups

The `user` and `group` resource types let us create and manage users and groups. There are differences between different operating systems as to what Puppet can do with the users and groups and how this works. The code in the following section is tested on Ubuntu, Linux. More information on the differences for users and groups on different platforms can be found on the Puppet website at http://docs.puppetlabs.com/references/latest/type.html#user.

Creating groups

The simplest way to create a group is simply to set the `ensure` parameter to `present`:

```
group { "wheel":
  ensure => "present",
}
```

Creating users

To create a user, the basic information we should provide is as follows:

- The username
- The fact that we want the user to exist (ensure => present)
- The group (gid) the user should be part of
- The shell to use for the user
- The home directory for the user
- If we want Puppet to manage the home directory for the user, in this case, it will create the folder for us if it does not exist
- The password for the user
- The requirements that we need the wheel group in place first

The code that will then create our user is as follows:

```
user { "developer":
  ensure => "present",
  gid => "wheel",
  shell => "/bin/bash",
  home => "/home/developer",
  managehome => true,
  password => "passwordtest",
  require => Group["wheel"]
}
```

Updating the sudoers file

It's all well and good being able to create users and groups on our machine, however, one thing that we can't do using the user and group resource types is define a user or group as having elevated privileges, unless we make the user a part of the root group.

We can use an exec command to push some text to the end of our sudoers file; the text we need to push just tells the file that we want to give the wheel group the sudo privileges, as shown in the following code:

```
exec { "/bin/echo \"%wheel  ALL=(ALL) ALL\" >> /etc/sudoers":
  require => Group["wheel"]
}
```

This code, however, will continually add this line to the file each time it is run, which we don't want, however, as we learned earlier, we can instruct the `exec` resources to only run at certain times. Thanks to `subscribe` and `refreshonly`:

```
exec { "/bin/echo \"%wheel    ALL=(ALL) ALL\" >> /etc/sudoers":
  subscribe => Group["wheel"],
  refreshonly => true
}
```

This still isn't ideal, as if we decide to *change* the `wheel` group then this would be rerun, so ideally, we might keep the `sudoers` file within our Puppet configuration instead and use Puppet to manage the changes to it.

Creating configurable classes

One limitation that our entire Puppet code has so far in this chapter is that with the exception of the contents of some files, the configuration is all fixed. If we want to reuse some of the Puppet code on another project, we might need to change things such as variable names, paths to files, or other project-or environment-specific properties.

To make our code more flexible, we can put the code into a class, and use class parameters to dynamically inject variables into the class.

A class is, at its simplest level, a method of grouping related code together; however, we can use them to build reusable and configurable modules. If we take the composer `Exec` resource illustrated earlier, we can start to make that reusable by putting it into a class:

```
class composer {
   exec{ "compose":
        command => '/bin/rm -rfv /var/www/repo/vendor/* && /bin/rm -f /var/www/repo/composer.lock && /usr/bin/curl -s http://getcomposer.org/installer | /usr/bin/php && cd /var/www/repo && /usr/bin/php /var/www/repo/composer.phar install',
        require => [ Package['curl'], Package['git-core'] ],
        creates => "/var/www/repo/composer.lock",
        timeout => 0
   }
}
```

While we can now more easily pull this into another project, we are locked down in terms of the location of the composer file and also other parameters that might be required. We also require two packages: we would either require that the developer adds these elsewhere to their Puppet code, or we would include them here, however, including them here would conflict with other modules and reduces flexibility. Class parameters let us pass information to a class when it is used; this information can be used to control the code within the class and also configure parts of the class.

For our `Composer` class, we might want to let the developer using it decide whether the dependencies are installed by the module or not, and also provide paths to be used by the module. Class parameters are defined in brackets immediately after the class name and can have default values, so if they are omitted, their defaults are used.

We can then use control statements to decide whether the dependencies should be installed, and we can pull in the contents of a variable using `${variable}`:

```
class composer ($install_deps = true, $path = '/var/www/repo/',
$composer_home = '/var/www/')   {

    if ($install_deps == true) {
        package { "curl":
            ensure => present
        }

        package { "git-core":
            ensure => present
        }
    }

    exec { "compose":
        command => "/bin/rm -rfv ${path}vendor/* && cd ${path} && /usr/bin/curl -s http://getcomposer.org/installer | /usr/bin/php && COMPOSER_HOME=\"${composer_home}\" /usr/bin/php ${path}composer.phar install",
        require => [ Package['curl'], Package['git-core'], Package['php5-cli'] ],
        creates => "${path}composer.lock",
        timeout => 0
    }
}
```

Now, when we want to use this class, we pass the values along with these variable names. Because of the way Puppet works, the ordering of the parameters doesn't mater; they are passed associatively with their corresponding variable names, as shown in the following code:

```
class {
    'composer':
        install_deps => true
}
```

Puppet modules

There are many existing, well-written, reusable Puppet modules freely available to use. Puppet Forge is a collection of modules, which is available at http://forge.puppetlabs.com/. It is always worth checking whether there is an existing module that solves your problem before writing your own.

Using Puppet to provision servers

We are going to take a look at how to use Puppet with Vagrant in *Chapter 6*, *Provisioning Vagrant Machines with Puppet, Ansible, and Chef*, however, Puppet can also be run independently. If Puppet is installed (it will be on most Vagrant base boxes, but if you want to run it on another machine, it might not be, so install it first), you can use the `apply` subcommand, passing with it the location of the `modules` folder and the default manifest to apply, as follows:

```
puppet apply --modulepath=/home/michael/provision/modules
    /home/michael/provision/manifests/default.pp
```

Summary

In this chapter, we had a whirlwind tour of Puppet and explored the various ways in which we could use it to provision a server for our projects. We installed software with the `Package` resource, managed cron jobs with the `Cron` resource, managed users and groups with the `User` and `Group` resources, and ran commands with the `Exec` resource. To manage execution order and dependency relationships with Puppet, we looked at using `Require`, `Subscribe`, `Notify`, and `Refreshonly`. We looked at how modules, classes, and stages work as well as how to use class parameters to configure reusable Puppet code. Finally, we looked at how to use Puppet to provision a machine.

In the next chapter, we will take a look at Ansible, another provisioning tool that has support built into Vagrant.

4
Using Ansible

Ansible is another provisioning tool supported by Vagrant that makes it easy for us to take a base operating system installation and turn it into a full-fledged server that suits the needs of our project.

In this chapter, we will quickly take a look at the basics of Ansible. We won't look at it within a Vagrant context just yet; we will simply take a look at how Ansible works, and how we can use it. In *Chapter 6, Provisioning Vagrant Machines with Puppet, Ansible, and Chef*, we will take a look at how to connect what we will learn in this chapter with Vagrant itself. In this chapter, we will learn the following topics:

- How Ansible works
- How to use Ansible to perform the following tasks:
    - Installing software
    - Managing files and folders within the filesystem
    - Managing cron jobs
    - Running commands
    - Managing users and groups
- How to use third-party Ansible roles
- How to manually run Ansible to provision a machine

Ansible itself is a large topic and subject of several books. For a more detailed look at Ansible, Packt Publishing has some titles dedicated to provisioning with Ansible:

- *Learning Ansible*: https://www.packtpub.com/networking-and-servers/learning-ansible
- *Ansible Configuration Management*: https://www.packtpub.com/networking-and-servers/ansible-configuration-management

Understanding Ansible

Ansible is an IT automation tool that provides provision, orchestration, and configuration management features. Unlike with Puppet and Chef, Ansible doesn't require any software to be preinstalled on the server, other than an SSH service, as the heavy lifting is done by our own computer that connects to our Ansible-managed servers and instructs the server on how it needs to change.

Like Puppet and Chef, Ansible is also idempotent. This means each time we run Ansible, it will only perform actions where a change is required—so if we install the Nginx web server, the first run of Ansible will install it and subsequent runs won't because it knows Nginx is already installed.

Ansible configuration is written in **Yaml Ain't Markup Language (YAML)**, which makes the configuration easy to read and write.

Conceptually, Ansible configuration is made up of **playbooks** that are made up of **plays**, which are made up of **tasks**. A playbook is the configuration for an entire system or environment, which is mapped to specific servers or hosts through plays—different plays can be applied to different groups of servers at different times from the same playbook. Each play contains a number of tasks, which, in turn, make calls to Ansible modules. In a more advanced context, we can make use of roles within Ansible (reusable functionality) such that our playbooks might simply be a mapping of hosts to roles. However, for the purposes of this chapter, we will put tasks and module calls directly in our playbook.

Modules within Ansible are similar in context to resources within Puppet. There are modules to deal with many different kinds of operations on a server, which we will discuss shortly.

Installing Ansible

Because Ansible doesn't require any software to be installed on the server side, we can't simply connect to a Vagrant virtual machine and try out Ansible because it isn't installed on there! In order to use it, both to try it out, and also when it comes to integrating with Vagrant, we need to install Ansible on our own computer, which is known as the control machine.

Although Ansible can be used to manage Windows Servers, it cannot be run from a Windows control machine.

Packages are available for many Linux distributions, and Ansible can be installed on OS X using Homebrew or Python's pip. Complete details of the different operating systems are available online at `http://docs.ansible.com/intro_installation.html`.

> Although we don't need anything installed on the server being managed, we *do need* SSH access to the machine, and unless we install additional plugins for Ansible, we will *also need* to have *public and private keys set up*, so that we can connect to the machine we wish to manage over SSH without a password from our control machine.

Creating an inventory

When we run Ansible to provision or configure a machine, Ansible takes the hosts we want to apply the configuration to, from our playbooks. It then looks up these machines in its inventory, which specify the addresses and connection details for these machines, so that Ansible can connect to them in order to check their status and run the provisioning tasks.

At a minimum, the inventory needs to contain a name and an IP address for each server that we want Ansible to manage. However, there are additional configurations we can provide, for example, setting the user to connect as, the password to use (which requires additional configuration), the port to connect through, and if we need to tunnel to the server through another. An example of creating an inventory is as follows:

```
default ansible_ssh_host=192.168.100.123
```

Although we are looking at Ansible outside the context of Vagrant, we still might want to use Ansible, independently, to connect to and configure a Vagrant-managed virtual machine so that we can test it in isolation. In *Chapter 6, Provisioning Vagrant Machines with Puppet, Ansible, and Chef*, we will learn how to do this within Vagrant itself. If we do this, we need to provide the port. We might also wish to change the user that we connect as to root, and ensure that a specific SSH key is used for the connection as follows:

```
default ansible_ssh_host=127.0.0.1 ansible_ssh_port=2222 ansible_ssh_user=root ansible_ssh_private_key=~/.ssh/id_rsa
```

This inventory file is simply a plain text file saved somewhere on our control machine. By default, Ansible will look for a file called /etc/ansible/hosts, which it expects to be the inventory, however, when we run Ansible, we can point to our own inventory file elsewhere, which we will do later in this chapter.

Creating Ansible playbooks

As we discussed, an Ansible playbook is a YAML file. The following example is a simple playbook that contains instructions to update the **Apt package manager** class on the machine called by default in our inventory:

```
---
- hosts: default
  tasks:
  - name: update apt cache
    apt: update_cache=yes
```

We can run this playbook by running the `ansible-playbook our-playbook.yml -i our-inventory-file` command. Ansible will then look up that this playbook is to be applied to the default machine, the default machine's details, connect to it, and if appropriate, run the command. We will walk through the execution process shortly.

Tasks are executed in the order that they appear within the playbook. However, we have the option to call other tasks to be run later once an action is completed, through the use of handlers, which we will discuss shortly.

> Because playbooks are written in YAML, the format and spacing/indentation in these files is critical. Incorrect indentation can cause files to not be parsed correctly.

Modules – what Ansible can do

Ansible modules are similar to Puppet resources, and we can use them to install and manage packages, servers, users, files, cron jobs, and so on.

The modules available include:

- **Apt**: This is used to manage apt packages
- **Git**: This is used to manage and deploy from git repositories
- **Service**: This is used to manage running services on the server
- **Copy**: This is used to copy files

Each module can be configured with different properties, as we will discuss in this chapter. A complete list of the modules is available from the Ansible website at `http://docs.ansible.com/list_of_all_modules.html`.

Installing software

Let's say we want to install Nginx on our server. There are three steps involved in this process:

1. Updating our package manager.
2. Installing the `nginx` package.
3. Running the `nginx` service.

Updating our package manager

We can use the `apt` module (http://docs.ansible.com/apt_module.html) to update the apt package manager's cache, which is the equivalent of performing an `apt-get update` command:

```
- name: update apt cache
  apt: update_cache=yes
```

The `update_cache` parameter can also be provided when we run other apt-related tasks, so instead of a dedicated task for it, we can instead specify that when we install Nginx, the package manager's cache must be up to date.

Installing the nginx package

We can use the `apt` module (http://docs.ansible.com/apt_module.html) to ensure that Nginx is installed, and if it isn't, it will be installed as follows:

```
- name: ensure nginx is installed
  apt: pkg=nginx state=present update_cache=yes
```

Here, we told Ansible to ensure that the state of the `nginx` package is present, and that we should update the package manager's cache before installing it. There are different states available, including the latest states to ensure that we have the latest version of a package present, or absent to ensure that a package is not installed on the server.

Running the nginx service

Finally, to make sure that Nginx is running, we use the `service` module. While Nginx will automatically run when we install it, we can connect to our new server and alter settings or services by mistake. If this happens, we can simply rerun the provisioner, as Nginx will already be installed, so it won't reinstall it, but the `service` module will force the server to start the `nginx` service. We can use the `enabled` parameter to ensure that the service is configured to start automatically when the system boots next:

```
- name: ensure nginx is running
  service: name=nginx state=started enabled=yes
```

Understanding file management

We can use the `file`, `copy`, and `template` modules within Ansible to manage files and folders within the filesystem. Let's take a look at some examples, which allow us to perform the following:

- Copy files
- Create symlinks
- Create folders

Copying a file

One common file operation we might want to perform would be to take a configuration file from our project and copy it into our virtual machine. One particular use case would be an Nginx configuration file; we might want to define some virtual hosts and other settings in a file, which we can share with our colleagues.

> While this works well and can get us up and running quickly, there are roles out there that allow us to configure Nginx and other software directly from Ansible. This typically works by the role of storing a template file (a copy of the configuration file with placeholders in it) and then, inserting data that we define within our playbook into the template, and copying the file onto the machine. However, for the sake of this introductory chapter, we will just copy a file across.

The `template` module (http://docs.ansible.com/template_module.html) allows us to copy a file from our control machine onto the machine being provisioned as follows:

```
- name: write the nginx config file
  template: src=nginx-default-site.conf dest=/etc/nginx/sites-
available/default.conf owner=www-data group=www-data
```

As this is our Nginx configuration file, it makes sense for us to reload or restart Nginx when this file changes to ensure that the updated configuration is applied to the server. We do this in two stages:

1. We set our task to notify a handler once it is done.
2. We create a handler, which is only activated when it is notified, to restart Nginx.

The following is a playbook that updates the apt cache, installs Nginx, ensures that the service is running, copies the configuration file, and then ensures that Nginx is restarted when that file changes through a `notify` operation and a handler. The `notify` and `handlers` code sections are highlighted are follows:

```
---
- hosts: default
  tasks:
  - name: update apt cache
    apt: update_cache=yes
  - name: ensure nginx is installed
    apt: pkg=nginx state=present
  - name: write the nginx config file
    template: src=nginx-default-site.conf dest=/etc/nginx/sites-available/default.conf
    notify:
    - restart nginx
  - name: ensure nginx is running
    service: name=nginx state=started
  handlers:
    - name: restart nginx
      service: name=nginx state=restarted
```

Creating a symlink

The `file` module (http://docs.ansible.com/file_module.html) allows us to create symbolic links to the existing files and folders in the filesystem. If, for instance, we want to map a public folder within our web servers root directory to a folder within our Vagrant shared folder, we can do this as follows:

```
- name: make our Vagrant synced folder our web root
  file: src=/vagrant dest=/var/www/site owner=www-data group=www-data state=link
```

Creating folders

We can also use the `file` resource type to create folders; this is particularly useful for scenarios such as folders to hold files (avatars, attachments, and so on) uploaded by users of a web application:

```
- name: create an uploads folder
   file: path=/var/www/uploads owner=www-data group=www-data mode=0777 state=directory
```

We can use the `mode` parameter to set the permissions of the folder, and the `owner` and `group` parameters to set the user and groups who own the directory (these also can be used for files we create and manage too). Finally, the `state` parameter is used to ensure that the path provided is a folder.

Managing cron

The `cron` module (http://docs.ansible.com/cron_module.html) lets us use Ansible to manage cron jobs, which we need to run on the machine. We provide a name (which is a required parameter), in this case, `web_cron`, the command to run, the user to run the command, and the times at which to run the command, as shown in the following code:

```
- name: Run some cron
   cron: name="web_cron" hour="1-4" minute="0,30" job="/usr/bin/php /vagrant/cron.php"
```

Ansible provides us with various different configuration options to define the times at which a cron should be run. These include:

- **Hour**: This value is between 0 and 23 inclusive
- **Minute**: This value is between 0 and 59 inclusive
- **Month**: This value is between 1 and 12 inclusive
- **Day**: This value is between 1 and 31 inclusive
- **Weekday**: This value is from Sunday (0) to Saturday (6)

If one of these is omitted from the configuration, then Ansible runs it for each one of the available options (that is, if we omit month, it will run for January through to December), as it has a default value of `*`. When defining the dates and times, we can either provide a range, for example, 1-5 or specifics, such as 1,2,10,12.

Running commands

The `command` and `shell` modules allow us to run commands through the terminal on the machine we are provisioning. The difference between the two is that the `shell` module will run the commands through a shell on the remote system. So if we need to access environment variables or operators, such as &, |, >, and <, then we need to use the `shell` module.

Managing users and groups

The `user` and `group` modules (http://docs.ansible.com/user_module.html and http://docs.ansible.com/group_module.html) let us create and manage users and groups.

Creating groups

We simply provide a name. By default, the `state` parameter is set to `present`:

```
- name: create some new group
  group: name=newgroup state=present
```

Creating users

To create a user we can use the `user` module (http://docs.ansible.com/user_module.html); the minimum information we need again is the username. However, we can also specify their group, password (providing a crypted hash as per http://docs.ansible.com/faq.html#how-do-i-generate-crypted-passwords-for-the-user-module), and even whether an SSH key can be generated if the user does not have one:

```
- name: create a new user
  user: name=ournewuser group=newgroup state=present
```

Using Ansible roles

There are many existing, well-written, reusable Ansible roles freely available to use. These roles typically manage large aspects of server functionality in one reusable bundle, for example, there is an Nginx role to manage Nginx and configure sites with it. There are many roles available on Ansible Galaxy (https://galaxy.ansible.com/), so it is worth checking these out before writing our own code!

Using Ansible to provision servers

Once we have a playbook and inventory file, we can run the `ansible-playbook` command to analyze our playbook, and ensure that the configuration for the matching servers in our inventory file is updated:

```
ansible-playbook our-playbook.yml -i our-inventory-file
```

When this command was run for the first time against a particular server, the output was something like this:

```
Michaels-iMac:packt-vagrant-2 michael$ ansible-playbook play.yml -i inventory

PLAY [default] ********************************************************

GATHERING FACTS *******************************************************
ok: [default]

TASK: [ensure nginx is installed] *************************************
changed: [default]

TASK: [write the nginx config file] ***********************************
changed: [default]

TASK: [ensure nginx is running] ***************************************
ok: [default]

NOTIFIED: [restart nginx] *********************************************
changed: [default]

PLAY RECAP ************************************************************
default                    : ok=5    changed=3    unreachable=0    failed=0

Michaels-iMac:packt-vagrant-2 michael$
```

Let's walk through this screenshot to see what is going on:

1. First, Ansible pulls the files together and checks whether everything is valid.
2. Next, it gathers facts about the related machines it needs to connect to. This is done by connecting over SSH and finding out information, such as specification, networking details, and so on.
3. Next, it runs through the tasks in our playbook. When installing and writing our configuration files, Ansible needs to make a change, because it isn't installed and the file isn't there.

4. Once installed, Nginx automatically starts, so the task to ensure that it is running doesn't do anything (this comes back to the idempotency of Ansible). As the configuration file writing notifies the handler to restart Nginx, Nginx is then restarted at the end.
5. Finally, we see a recap, three changes were made, and five tasks resulted in an **ok** response.

On subsequent runs, the output looks like this:

```
Michaels-iMac:packt-vagrant-2 michael$ ansible-playbook play.yml -i inventory

PLAY [default] ********************************************************

GATHERING FACTS *******************************************************
ok: [default]

TASK: [ensure nginx is installed] *************************************
ok: [default]

TASK: [write the nginx config file] ***********************************
ok: [default]

TASK: [ensure nginx is running] ***************************************
ok: [default]

PLAY RECAP ************************************************************
default                    : ok=4    changed=0    unreachable=0    failed=0

Michaels-iMac:packt-vagrant-2 michael$
```

There are two differences: firstly, Ansible doesn't need to do anything, so everything is green and we get four **ok** results. Again, this is because Ansible is idempotent, so it only does things when a change to the system is required. Secondly, because we didn't notify the Nginx restart handler, the handler wasn't even run as a task, which is why our recap number has dropped to 4, and there was no related output for the handler.

Summary

In this chapter, we learned about Ansible, the IT automation tool. We looked at how it works, and how to create an inventory file so Ansible can manage different servers, and how to write playbooks, which can work with some of the different modules.

We installed the software and learned to update the package manager cache with the `apt` module, and packages that are services were then started and managed with the `service` module. The `template` module allowed us to copy files from our control machine to the Ansible-managed machine. In order to trigger service reloads, we looked into notifying handlers after specific tasks occur.

To create and manage, files, folders, and symlinks the `file` module was used, and we used the `cron` module to create and manage cron jobs. Users and groups were created and managed with the `user` and `group` modules and finally we looked into running commands with the `command` and `shell` modules.

In the next chapter, we will take a look at Chef, the final provisioner that we will discuss in this book, and also discuss how we can use it to provision servers.

5
Using Chef

Chef is another provisioning tool supported by Vagrant that makes it easy for us to take a base operating system installation and turn it into a full-fledged server suited to the needs of our project.

In this chapter, we will quickly take a look at the basics of Chef. We won't look at it within a Vagrant context just yet; we will simply take a look at how Chef works, and how we can use it. In *Chapter 6, Provisioning Vagrant Machines with Puppet, Ansible, and Chef*, we will take a look at how to connect what we will learn in this chapter with Vagrant itself. In this chapter, we will learn the following topics:

- How Chef works
- The basics behind Chef cookbooks and recipes
- How to use Chef to perform the following tasks:
    - Installing software
    - Managing files and folders within the filesystem
    - Managing cron jobs
    - Running commands
    - Managing users and groups
- How to use third-party Chef cookbooks and recipes
- How to manually run Chef to provision a machine

Chef itself is a large topic and the subject of several books. For a more detailed look at Chef, Packt Publishing has some titles dedicated to provisioning with Chef:

- *Chef Infrastructure Automation Cookbook*, http://www.packtpub.com/chef-infrastructure-automation-cookbook/book
- *Instant Chef Starter*, http://www.packtpub.com/chef-starter/book

Knowing about Chef

Chef is a provisioning tool that we can use to set up a server for use for a project. The configuration, which determines how the server needs to be set up, can be stored within our Vagrant project and can be shared with teammates through version control, ensuring that everyone gets an up-to-date copy of the required development environment.

Information about how a server should be configured, that is, its software, files, users, and groups, is written into files known as Chef recipes. These recipes are written as Ruby files. Chef takes this information and matches it to providers that are used to execute the configuration on the machine in a compatible way.

For our purposes, we will use Chef-solo, which is its standalone mode (this is also how Vagrant uses it). Chef-solo means that everything runs from one machine. Chef also has client-server capabilities, where you can define the Chef cookbooks and roles for all the servers in your infrastructure on a central host, and it keeps your individual servers at the required level of configuration.

As with Puppet, Chef is also idempotent, which means running Chef on a machine multiple times has the same effect as running it only once.

Creating cookbooks and recipes with Chef

Chef instructions are recipes that are bundled together in cookbooks. A cookbook contains at least one recipe, which performs some actions. Cookbooks can contain multiple recipes and other resources such as templates and files.

At its most basic level, a cookbook is a folder (named as the name of the cookbook) that contains at least a `recipes` folder, which contains at least a default recipe file, `default.rb`. Files are typically stored in a `files` folder within the `cookbook` folder and template files within the `templates` folder.

While both Puppet and Chef use Ruby, Puppet is a domain-specific language, which makes it look and feel like its own language, whereas Chef is structured more like Ruby itself.

Resources – what Chef can do

Chef uses resources to define the actions and operations that can be performed against the system. Resources are mapped to a Chef code, which varies depending on the platform/operating system being used. For example, on an Ubuntu machine, the package resource is mapped to `apt-get`. Some of these system-specific instructions can also be accessed directly via their own resources, `apt_package`. For example, this is used to manage packages on Ubuntu- and Debian-based systems, whereas using the package resource, Chef will work out which package manager to use based on the operating system.

Resource types available include:

- `cron`: This resource type is used to manage cron jobs on Linux- and Unix-based systems
- `execute`: This resource type is used to run commands at the terminal/command prompt
- `file`: This resource type is used to manage and manipulate files and folders on the filesystem
- `group`: This resource type is used to manage user groups
- `package`: This resource type is used to install software
- `service`: This resource type is used to manage running services on the machine
- `template`: This resource type is used to manage file contents with an embedded Ruby template
- `user`: This resource type is used to manage user accounts on the machine

Each resource can be configured with different attributes, as we will discuss in this chapter. A complete list of the resource types is available on the Opscode website (Opscode is the company behind Chef) at `http://docs.opscode.com/resource.html`.

Installing software

Let's say we want to install Nginx on our server. There are three steps involved in this process:

1. Updating our package manager.
2. Installing the `nginx` package.
3. Running the `nginx` service.

Because the first step is different depending on the operating system we are running, we might want to move this out of Chef at a later stage; however, we will use it within Chef for the time being. Any operating specific commands (such as this) are written for Ubuntu, which is the operating system we are using with Vagrant.

Updating our package manager

In order to update our package manager, we need to run a command on the server. This can be achieved using the `execute` resource within Chef as follows:

```
execute "apt-get update" do
  ignore_failure true
end
```

This instructs Chef to run the `apt-get update` command. As the name of the resource (the part provided in quotes after the name of the resource) is the command we want to run, this will be executed. If we use a friendly name instead, then we would need to provide a command attribute as follows:

```
execute "update-package-manager" do
  command "apt-get update"
  ignore_failure true
end
```

By default, the `execute` resources have a timeout of 3,600 seconds, however, this can be overridden by giving a `timeout` attribute to the resource and a time value, for example:

```
execute "apt-get update" do
  ignore_failure true
  timeout 6000
end
```

Installing the nginx package

We can use the `package` resource to ensure that Nginx is installed, and if it isn't, it will be installed as follows:

```
package "nginx" do
  action :install
end
```

Here, we told Chef to ensure that the `nginx` package is installed. Provided that we have included the recipe or cookbook that contains the `apt-get update` command before the preceding code, our package manager will be up to date.

Running the nginx service

Finally, to make sure that Nginx is running, we use the `service` resource. As well as ensuring Nginx runs when it is first installed, this also ensures that if we make any changes to our server (and accidentally stop Nginx), we can simply rerun the provisioner. As Nginx will already be installed it won't reinstall it, but the `service` resource will force Chef to enable the `nginx` service (so it automatically starts on system boot), and start the service when the command is run, as follows:

```
service "nginx" do
  supports :status => true, :restart => true, :reload => true
    action [ :enable, :start ]
end
```

The `supports` property is a list of attributes that instruct Chef on how to manage a particular service. The action ensures that we enable the service (to have it run when the machine boots up) and run the service (so, we don't have to wait for a restart).

Understanding file management

We can use `cookbook_file`, `directory`, `link`, and `template` resources within Chef to manage files and folders within the filesystem. Let's take a look at some examples, which allow us to:

- Copy files
- Create symlinks
- Create folders
- Create multiple folders in one go

Copying a file

One common file operation we might want to perform would be to take a configuration file from our project and copy it into our virtual machine. One particular use case would be an Nginx configuration file; we might want to define some virtual hosts and other settings in a file, which we can share with our colleagues.

> While this works well and can get us up and running quickly, there are modules out there that allow us to configure Nginx and other software directly from Chef. This typically works by the module storing a template file (a copy of the configuration file with placeholders in it) and then inserting data we define within Chef into the template as well as copying the file onto the machine. However, for the sake of this introductory chapter, we will just copy a file across.

The `cookbook_file` resource allows us to copy a file from a Chef cookbook onto the machine as follows:

```
cookbook_file "/etc/nginx/sites-available/default" do
  backup false
  action :create_if_missing
end
```

Because we omitted the source and path attributes, Chef makes some assumptions. It takes the basename (in effect, the last element) of the name and uses this as the source (the basename of /etc/nginx/sites-available/default being the default) and uses the name as the path (destination). The source file should be located in the `files` folder within the cookbook's own folder.

As this is an Nginx configuration file, it is worth ensuring that Nginx is already installed; otherwise, Nginx will override this when it installs the first time, and this wouldn't make the process idempotent. We can do this by notifying the `nginx` service, for example:

```
cookbook_file "/etc/nginx/sites-available/default" do
  backup false
  action :create_if_missing
  notifies :restart, "service[nginx]", :delayed

end
```

The `delayed` option allows all of these `restart` requests to be queued up and executed at the end of Chef's execution; the opposite of this being `immediately`.

Creating a symlink

The `link` resource allows us to create symbolic links to the existing files and folders on the filesystem. If, for instance, we want to map a `public` folder within our web server's root directory to a folder within our Vagrant `shared` folder, we can do this as follows:

```
link "/var/www/public" do
  to "/vagrant/src/public"
end
```

Creating folders

We can use the `directory` resource to create folders; this is particularly useful for scenarios such as folders to hold files (avatars, attachments, and so on) uploaded by users of a web application:

```
directory "/var/www/uploads" do
  owner "root"
  group "root"
  mode 00777
  action :create
end
```

We can use the `mode` parameter to set the permissions of the folder, and the `owner` and `group` parameters to set the user and groups who own the directory (these also can be used for files we create and manage too). Finally, the `:create` action is used to ensure that the folder is created.

Creating multiple folders in a single process with looping

In many web projects, we might need to create a number of folders within our servers or our Vagrant virtual machines. In particular, we might want to create a number of `cache` folders for different parts of our application, or we might want to create some `upload` folders.

In order to do this, we can simply create an array that contains all of the folders we want to create. We can then use the `directory` resource type and loop through a list of directory names:

```
%w{dir1 dir2 dir3}.each do |dir|
  directory "/tmp/mydirs/#{dir}" do
    mode 00777
    owner "www-data"
    group "www-data"
    action :create
  end
end
```

Managing cron

The `cron` resource type lets us use Chef to manage cron jobs that we need to run on the machine. We provide a name, in this case, `web_cron`, the command to run, the user to run the command, and the times at which to run the command, as shown in the following code:

```
cron "web_cron" do
  action :create
  command "/usr/bin/php /vagrant/cron.php"
    user "root"
  hour "1-4"
    minute "0,30"
end
```

Chef provides us with various different configuration options to define the times at which a cron should be run; these include:

- `hour`: This value is between 0 and 23 inclusive
- `minute`: This value is between 0 and 59 inclusive
- `month`: This value is between 1 and 12 inclusive
- `day`: This value is between 1 and 31 inclusive
- `weekday`: This value is Sunday (0) - Saturday (6)

If one of these is omitted from the configuration, then Chef runs it for each one of the available options (that is, if we omit month, it will run from January through to December). When defining the dates and times, we can either provide a range, for example, `1-5`, or specifics, such as `1,2,10,12`. We can also provide an `emailto` property to e-mail the resulting output from the cron to an e-mail address of our choice.

Running commands

The `execute` resource allows us to run commands through the terminal on the machine we are provisioning. One caveat with the `exec` command is that if you reprovision with Chef it will rerun the command, which can be damaging depending on the command. What we can do with the `execute` resource is set the `creates` parameter. The `creates` parameter tells Chef that a file will be created when the command is run; if Chef finds that file, it knows that it has already been run, and it won't run it again.

Take, for example, the following configuration; this would use the PHP composer tool to download dependencies. The command itself creates a file called `composer.lock` (we can, of course, use the `exec` command itself to create a file manually, perhaps using the `touch` command). Because of the lock file that is created, we can use the `creates` parameter to prevent the command from being executed multiple times when a lock file is found:

```
execute "compose" do
  command "/bin/rm -rfv /var/www/repo/vendor/* && /bin/rm -f
    /var/www/repo/composer.lock && /usr/bin/curl -s
      http://getcomposer.org/installer | /usr/bin/php && cd
        /var/www/repo && /usr/bin/php /var/www/repo/composer
          .phar install"
  creates "/var/www/repo/composer.lock"
  timeout 6000
end
```

Managing users and groups

The `user` and `group` resource types let us create and manage users and groups. There are differences between different operating systems as to what Chef can do with the users and groups and how this works.

Creating groups

The simplest way to create a group is simply to set the action to `:create`, as follows:

```
group "wheel" do
  action :create
end
```

Creating users

To create a user, we should provide the following basic information:

- The username
- The fact that we want to create the user
- The group (`gid`) the user should be part of
- The shell to use for the user
- The home directory for the user
- Whether we want Chef to manage the home directory for the user; in this case, it will create the folder for us if it does not exist
- The password for the user

The code that will then create our user is as follows:

```
user "developer" do
  action :create
  gid "wheel"
  shell "/bin/bash"
  home "/home/developer"
  supports {:manage_home => true}
  password "passwordtest"
end
```

Updating the sudoers file

It's all well and good being able to create users and groups on our machine, however, one thing that we can't do using the `user` and `group` resource types is define a user or group as having elevated privileges, unless we make the user a part of the root group.

We can use an `exec` command through the `execute` resource to push some text to the end of our `suoders` file; the text we need to push simply tells the file that we want to give the `wheel` group `sudo` privileges. The command we will need to execute is as follows:

```
/bin/echo \"%wheel  ALL=(ALL)  ALL\" >> /etc/sudoers
```

Knowing common resource functionalities

There is also a set of common functionality available to all resources. This common functionality includes:

- The ability to do nothing with the `:nothing` action
- Shared attributes available to all resources: `ignore_failure`, `provider`, `retries`, `retry_delay`, and `supports`
- The `not_if` and `only_if` conditions to ensure that actions only run when certain conditions are met; these are commands that are run and depending on their return value, recipes, and resources can be ignored
- There are notifications to instruct other resources that another action has been completed, or for a resource to take action if another resource changes (subscribes)

Using Chef cookbooks

There are many existing, well-written, reusable Chef cookbooks freely available to use. The Opscode community site contains a collection of them at `http://community.opscode.com/cookbooks`. It is always worth checking whether there is an existing cookbook that solves your problem before writing your own.

Using Chef to provision servers

We will take a look at how to use Chef with Vagrant in *Chapter 6, Provisioning Vagrant Machines with Puppet, Ansible, and Chef*; however, Chef can also be run in its own right. Provided Chef is installed (it will be on most Vagrant base boxes, but if you want to run it on another machine, it might not be, so install it first), you can use the `chef-solo` command, passing with it the location of a configuration file to use, and a JSON file that contains attributes we wish to use (this should include the rub list, which is the list of recipes and cookbooks we wish to use), as follows:

```
chef-solo -c /home/michael/chefconfig.rb -j
   /home/michael/attributes.json
```

There are some useful links in this list you can refer to for more information

- Chef-solo configuration: `http://docs.opscode.com/config_rb_solo.html`
- Apply recipes to run lists: `http://docs.chef.io/recipes.html#apply-to-run-lists`
- Anatomy of a Chef run: `https://github.com/jhotta/chef-fundamentals-ja/blob/master/slides/anatomy-of-a-chef-run/01_slide.md`
- Chef tutorial: `http://www.mechanicalfish.net/configure-a-server-with-chef-solo-in-five-minutes/`

Summary

In this chapter, we had a whirlwind tour of Chef and explored the various ways we could use it to provision a server for our projects. This included how to install software packages with the `package` resource and run services with the `service` resource. We also managed cron jobs with the `cron` resource, managed users and groups, and ran commands. Finally, we looked at how recipes and cookbooks work, and how we can use Chef to provision a server.

In the next chapter, we will take a look at how to use both Chef and Puppet to provision a machine within the context of Vagrant.

6
Provisioning Vagrant Machines with Puppet, Ansible, and Chef

In *Chapter 3*, *Provisioning with Puppet*, *Chapter 4*, *Using Ansible*, and *Chapter 5*, *Using Chef*, we had an introduction to Puppet, Chef, and Ansible, which are provisioning tools with support built into Vagrant. However, we only looked at how the tools worked in a general way; we didn't look at how to use them with Vagrant.

In this chapter, you will learn the following topics:

- Using Puppet within Vagrant
- Using Chef within Vagrant
- Using Ansible within Vagrant
- Recapping how to provision with the built-in SSH provisioner
- Working with multiple provisioners
- How we can override the provisioning tools through the command line

Provisioning within Vagrant

Vagrant relies on base boxes for the guest virtual machines; these are specifically preconfigured virtual machine images that have certain software packages preinstalled and preconfigured. Puppet and Chef are two such software packages that are preinstalled (Ansible is controlled by Vagrant itself on the *host machine*, so it isn't installed on the virtual machine, but requires an SSH connection to the virtual machine). Vagrant has its own interface through to these packages from the host machine. This means we can provide some configuration in our Vagrant file, and Vagrant will pass this information to the relevant provisioners on the guest VM.

Provisioning with Puppet on Vagrant

Vagrant supports two methods of using Puppet:

- Puppet in standalone mode using the `puppet apply` command on the VM
- Puppet in client/server mode, whereby the VM (using the Puppet agent) will be configured from a central server

Let's take a look at how to configure Vagrant with Puppet using these two different methods.

Using Puppet in standalone mode

Puppet standalone is the simplest way to use Puppet with Vagrant. We simply tell Vagrant where we have put our Puppet manifests and modules, and what manifest should be run. The smallest amount of configuration we need within our Vagrant file in order to use Puppet is this:

```
config.vm.provision "puppet" do |puppet|
end
```

This should go within the `Vagrant.configure("2") do |config| ... end` block of code within the Vagrant file.

Along with this configuration, we will need a Puppet manifest called `default.pp` in the `manifests` folder of our project root. Vagrant will then use this to provision the machine.

This will instruct Vagrant to run the Puppet provisioner either when the machine boots up for the first time or if we run the `vagrant provision` command. The default Vagrant Puppet setup will make the following assumptions, unless we override the settings:

- Manifests will be located in the `manifests` folder
- Modules will also be located in the `manifests` folder (we may want to point these elsewhere, especially if we are using third-party modules, to keep them separate)
- The manifest file to use will be `default.pp` (It will obviously be within the `manifests` folder; it can be useful to override this if we use Puppet modules and manifests within the same project for multiple environments. We may have a manifest for our Vagrant VM, one for our production environment and one for a user acceptance testing platform, for example.)

We can modify these options by provisioning configuration options, as opposed to just telling Vagrant to provision with Puppet. When creating projects that are managed by Vagrant, I like to put all my provision-related files within the `provision` folder. In order to override these, within the Puppet configuration for Vagrant, we can then specify options for the location of the Puppet manifests (`puppet.manifests_path`), the name of the Puppet manifest to apply (`puppet.manifests_file`), and the location of any Puppet modules, which we may reference within our Puppet manifest (`puppet.module_path`). The following customizes these options:

```
config.vm.provision "puppet" do |puppet|
  puppet.manifests_path = "provision/puppet/manifests"
  puppet.manifest_file  = "default.pp"
  puppet.module_path    = "provision/puppet/modules"
end
```

It is important for us to have the ability to at least change the manifest file, as Vagrant also supports a multi-VM environment, where a single project can have a number of virtual machines (for example, a web server and a database server). With this setup, we will need to tell Vagrant which manifest file to use for each of the machines, so that the web server can be properly configured as a web server and the database server as a database server.

Puppet provisioning in action

With the knowledge we gained of creating Puppet modules and manifests from *Chapter 3*, *Provisioning with Puppet*, we can now point our Vagrant configuration at these files, and see it in action. If we run a Vagrant file on a project, which is suitably configured, we will see the output of Puppet applying its settings to our virtual machine in the terminal window, as shown in the following screenshot:

```
notice: /Stage[veryfirst]/Dns/Exec[updatedns]/returns: executed successfully
notice: /Stage[veryfirst]/Dns/Exec[preparenetworking]/returns: executed successfully
notice: /Stage[ppa]/Misc/Exec[apt-get update]/returns: executed successfully
notice: /Stage[main]/Sudo/Exec[/bin/echo "%wheel ALL=(ALL) ALL" >> /etc/sudoers]/returns: executed successfully
notice: /Stage[main]/Php/Package[php5-mhash]/ensure: ensure changed 'purged' to 'present'
notice: /Stage[main]/Mysql/Package[libmysqlclient15-dev]/ensure: ensure changed 'purged' to 'present'
notice: /Stage[main]/Mysql/Exec[apache2ctl graceful]/returns: executed successfully
notice: /Stage[main]/Php/Exec[testing-and-qa]/returns: executed successfully
notice: /Stage[main]/Mail/Exec[autostartmail]/returns: executed successfully
notice: /Stage[last]/Modrewrite/Exec[enabledmodrewrite]/returns: executed successfully
notice: /Stage[last]/Modrewrite/Exec[reload-apache2-again]/returns: executed successfully
notice: Finished catalog run in 382.39 seconds
Michaels-MacBook-Pro:template michael$
```

The console output highlights details of each Puppet instruction that is run, including:

- The stage the instruction is within (this is the Puppet stage, as we discussed in *Chapter 3*, *Provisioning with Puppet*, which allows us to group classes together to control the ordering of certain actions)
- The module
- The resource type
- The resource name
- Whether the instruction was executed successfully

Using Puppet in client/server mode

As discussed earlier, we can also run Puppet within our Vagrant environment in client/server mode using the Puppet agent on the virtual machine. The configuration required for this is minimal; we simply tell Vagrant the address of the Puppet server we are using and the name of our node (the virtual machine we are setting up):

```
config.vm.provision "puppet_server" do |puppet|
  puppet.puppet_server = "puppet.internal.michaelpeacock.co.uk"
  puppet.puppet_node = "vm.internal.michaelpeacock.co.uk"
end
```

The node name is the reference for the machine within the Puppet server, so the Puppet server knows how our VM should be configured. The node name is also used to generate an SSL certificate so that the VM can authenticate with the Puppet server (more details on this are available on the Puppet website, puppetlabs.com, and the Puppet blog, puppetlabs.com/blog/deploying-puppet-in-client-server-standalone-and-massively-scaled-environments/.

Provisioning with Ansible on Vagrant

In order to use Ansible within a Vagrant project, we need to tell Vagrant where the playbook and inventory files are:

```
config.vm.provision "ansible" do |ansible|
  ansible.playbook = "provision/ansible/playbook.yml"
end
```

Ansible needs to know which machines to provision; unlike with other provisioners, where this is explicitly known from the Vagrantfile configuration, Ansible uses an `inventory` file to configure this. The `inventory` file contains a list of environment names and IP addresses; we use this file to restrict which commands Ansible runs on specific environments. We can omit this file, and Vagrant will generate one for all of the virtual machines it manages for us in the current project.

We can also create our own `inventory` file. At a minimum, it needs to know the name of the virtual machine (from our Vagrantfile) and the IP address. To provide only these two pieces of information, this requires the virtual machine to be running on its own IP address (per the Vagrantfile networking configuration):

```
default ansible_ssh_host=10.11.100.123
```

Alternatively, we can provide the SSH port to use, so that Ansible can connect from our host machine to our virtual machine:

```
default ansible_ssh_host=127.0.0.1 ansible_ssh_port=2222
```

To tell Vagrant and Ansible about our own custom `inventory` file, we need to add it to our Vagrantfile as follows:

```
config.vm.provision "ansible" do |ansible|
  ansible.playbook = "provision/ansible/playbook.yml"
  ansible.inventory_file = "provision/ansible/inventory"
end
```

Provisioning with Chef on Vagrant

Vagrant also supports two methods of using Chef:

- Chef-solo
- Chef in client/server mode with Chef client

Let's take a look at how to configure Vagrant with Chef using these two different methods.

Using Chef-solo

Chef-solo is the Chef equivalent of Puppet standalone.

The simplest way to use this within our project is simply to provide a Chef run list to Vagrant; this tells Vagrant which cookbooks should be applied. The following is an example of telling Vagrant to use the PHP cookbook:

```
config.vm.provision "chef_solo" do |chef|
  chef.add_recipe "php"
end
```

This takes the PHP cookbook from the default `cookbooks` folder and applies it to the virtual machine.

As with Puppet, Vagrant makes some assumptions by default; they are as follows:

- Cookbooks are stored in the `cookbooks` folder within the project root. The `chef.cookbooks_path` setting allows us to override the `cookbooks` folder location. We can either provide a single path or an array of paths (wrapped in square brackets, separated with commas) if we want Vagrant and Chef to look in a range of folders for our cookbooks. The following code will go into our Vagrant file to tell Vagrant to override the `cookbooks` folder with `provision/cookbooks`:

  ```
  config.vm.provision "chef_solo" do |chef|
    chef.cookbooks_path = "provision/cookbooks"
  end
  ```

- We can also use Chef roles by providing:
    - The location of the `roles` folder
    - The roles we wish to add to the VM

  More information on Chef roles can be found on the Opscode website (`http://docs.opscode.com/essentials_roles.html`).

  The following code in our Vagrant file will set up our project to use Chef roles:

  ```
  config.vm.provision "chef_solo" do |chef|
    chef.roles_path = "provision/roles"
    chef.add_role("web")
  end
  ```

Using Chef in client/server mode

Like Puppet, Chef also has a client/server method to provision machines using Chef client on the VM. To use Chef client, we need to tell Vagrant where the Chef server is located (through the `chef.chef_server_url` setting), and provide the authorization key that will be used to authenticate the VM with the server (through the `chef.validation_key_path` setting).

The following code in our Vagrant file will instruct Vagrant to provision from a Chef server:

```
config.vm.provision "chef_client" do |chef|
  chef.chef_server_url = "http://chef.internal.michaelpeacock.
    co.uk:4000/" chef.validation_key_path = "key.pem"
end
```

We can also override the run list that the Chef server provides for our VM by manually adding roles and recipes to this configuration. If we have specified different environments on our Chef server, we can specify which environment we want to use with the `chef.environment` configuration.

> Vagrant VMs that use Chef server will have the corresponding node and client entries on the Chef server, which is named with the hostname of the VM. If we destroy the VM and recreate it, Chef will generate an error because the client and node entries are already present on the server. We need to remove these from the Chef server when we destroy a VM. This can be done using the `knife` tool from Chef, `knife node delete our-vm-hostname && knife client delete our-vm-hostname`.

Provisioning with SSH – a recap

As we discussed in *Chapter 2*, *Managing Vagrant Boxes and Projects*, we can instruct Vagrant to run a series of SSH commands on the VM. This can be used to provision the server.

There are two ways to use SSH provisioning:

- **Path**: This provides a file to execute
- **Inline**: This is used to provide specific commands to run

Both of these are shown as follows:

```
config.vm.provision "shell", path: "provision/setup.sh"
config.vm.provision "shell", inline: "apt-get install apache2"
```

Using multiple provisioners on a single project

We can use multiple provisioners within a single project if we wish; we simply need to put them in the order we wish for them to be executed within our Vagrant file. The following command will first run an SSH command before provisioning with Puppet:

```
Vagrant.configure("2") do |config|
  Config.vm.box = "ubuntu/trusty64"

  config.vm.provision "shell", inline: "apt-get update"

  config.vm.provision "puppet" do |puppet|
      puppet.manifests_path = "provision/puppet/manifests"
      puppet.manifest_file  = "default.pp"
      puppet.module_path = "provision/puppet/modules"
  end

end
```

Using multiple provisioners can be useful, especially if one is more suited at specific tasks than another, or if we require some prerequisites. For example, when using Puppet and Chef in client/server mode, they need to have an SSH key to communicate with the server. We can use a shell provisioner to instruct the VM to download the keys we prepared from a secure location, before the Puppet or Chef provisioners kick in.

Overriding provisioning via the command line

There may be instances where we want to restrict or enforce the execution of provisioning or even a specific provisioner within a project. The following commands are all executed from the host machine:

- We can cancel a running provision by pressing *CMD + C* at the terminal.
- We can instruct Vagrant to rerun provisioning on a VM using the `vagrant provision` command.
- We can also add `--no-provision` to the `up` command to instruct Vagrant to not run the provisioning tools when performing the `up` action, for example, `vagrant up --no-provision`.

- By default, Vagrant will only provision when it first boots a machine. For subsequent boots of an existing machine, Vagrant knows that the machines are configured, and it will not provision them. We can override this with the `--provision` option, for example, `vagrant up --provision`.
- We can also provision with just a specific provisioner should we wish, for example, if we want to instruct Vagrant to just run Puppet in standalone mode (in a project that has multiple provisioners configured), we need to run `vagrant provision --provision-with=puppet`.

Summary

In this chapter, we learned how we can apply our knowledge of Puppet and Chef from *Chapter 3, Provisioning with Puppet*, *Chapter 4, Using Ansible*, and *Chapter 5, Using Chef*, and configure Vagrant to use these tools to provision our virtual machines.

We started off by learning to use Puppet in standalone mode that uses the `puppet apply` command to apply locally stored manifests and modules onto the machine. Then, we continued using Puppet in the client/server mode that uses the Puppet agent to retrieve the configuration from a central server to provision the machine.

We then learned how to use Ansible to run playbooks on specific machines along with the fundamentals of Chef-solo, which applies locally stored cookbooks and recipes to the machine. It also included the usage of Chef in client/server mode, which uses the Chef client to retrieve the configuration from a central server to provision the machine.

Other standard provisioners were also checked using SSH provisioning and multiple provisioning options for the same project. Finally, we rounded off by running multiple provisioners within a single project, overriding provisioning on the command line and rerunning the provisioning tools with `vagrant provision`.

Now, we have fully mastered how to set up, use, and manage Vagrant along with the provisioning tools to work on a single machine project. In *Chapter 7, Working with Multiple Machines*, we will take a look at how to use Vagrant and our knowledge of provisioners to manage a multimachine project, with provisioners configuring different machines for different purposes for use within the project, for example, a web server and a database server.

7
Working with Multiple Machines

So far, we have seen how we can get Vagrant to a stage where our development environment is contained in Vagrant-managed virtual machines, with one of the key aspects being that these virtual machines mimic our production environment. It gives us the flexibility of being able to encapsulate the development environment for different projects so that we can easily switch from one to another without having to modify the software on our own machines.

In many cases, the features we learned so far are enough. However, web projects are becoming more and more complex, with developers continually improving, having to deal with multiple machines in their architecture to help with scalability and stability. While it can be said that scalability and stability issues won't impact our development environment (as we won't have huge amounts of traffic coming to our development environment, unless we load-test it), we want to ensure that the coupling between servers within our code (such as application code connecting to a remote database) works in our development environment before we put the project online.

Thankfully, Vagrant has support for running multiple virtual machines at the same time within the same project. We can use this to test multimachine architectures and distributed systems on our own local machine before we share our changes with colleagues in a staging environment, and before the project goes live. Replicating a multimachine environment in development greatly helps us improve the reliability of our projects and instills confidence in the work that we do.

In this chapter, we will learn the following topics:

- How to run multiple virtual machines within a single Vagrant project
- How to provide different distinct configuration to these virtual machines, including the following:
    - Names
    - IP addresses on a private network so that they can communicate with one another
    - Base boxes
    - Provisioning
    - Shared folders
- How to connect to the different virtual machines over SSH without having to know or remember their IP addresses

Using multiple machines with Vagrant

In order to use multiple virtual machines within our project, we need to tell Vagrant about them, and we need to provide additional configuration for the individual virtual machines.

Defining multiple virtual machines

Within the standard Vagrant project configuration file, we can tell Vagrant that we wish to assign a name to a virtual machine being managed by the project. Within this subconfiguration, we provide the information Vagrant needs that is specific to that VM.

The syntax for the subconfigurations is as follows:

```
config.vm.define :name_of_the_vm do |name_of_the_vm|
    #configuration specific to the virtual machine
end
```

This is applied to a project that requires two virtual machines, named `server1` and `server2`, both running the `precise64` box:

```ruby
# -*- mode: ruby -*-
# vi: set ft=ruby :

VAGRANTFILE_API_VERSION = "2"

Vagrant.configure(VAGRANTFILE_API_VERSION) do |config|

  config.vm.define :server1 do |server1|
    server1.vm.box = "hashicorp/precise64"
  end

  config.vm.define :server2 do |server2|
    server2.vm.box = "hashicorp/precise64"
  end

end
```

Connecting to the multiple virtual machines over SSH

When our multiple machines boot up in our multimachine project, Vagrant automatically maps different ports from our host machine to the SSH ports on the various guest machines.

Working with Multiple Machines

Let's take a look at the console output when booting a Vagrant project with two virtual machines within it:

```
Michaels-MBP:packt-vagrant-book michael$ vagrant up
Bringing machine 'server1' up with 'virtualbox' provider...
Bringing machine 'server2' up with 'virtualbox' provider...
==> server1: Importing base box 'hashicorp/precise64'...
==> server1: Matching MAC address for NAT networking...
==> server1: Checking if box 'hashicorp/precise64' is up to date...
==> server1: Setting the name of the VM: packt-vagrant-book_server1_1414969672940_91863
==> server1: Clearing any previously set network interfaces...
==> server1: Preparing network interfaces based on configuration...
    server1: Adapter 1: nat
    server1: Adapter 2: hostonly
==> server1: Forwarding ports...
    server1: 22 => 2222 (adapter 1)
==> server1: Booting VM...
==> server1: Waiting for machine to boot. This may take a few minutes...
    server1: SSH address: 127.0.0.1:2222
    server1: SSH username: vagrant
    server1: SSH auth method: private key
    server1: Warning: Connection timeout. Retrying...
==> server1: Machine booted and ready!
==> server1: Checking for guest additions in VM...
    server1: The guest additions on this VM do not match the installed version of
    server1: VirtualBox! In most cases this is fine, but in rare cases it can
    server1: prevent things such as shared folders from working properly. If you see
    server1: shared folder errors, please make sure the guest additions within the
    server1: virtual machine match the version of VirtualBox you have installed on
    server1: your host and reload your VM.
    server1:
    server1: Guest Additions Version: 4.2.0
    server1: VirtualBox Version: 4.3
==> server1: Configuring and enabling network interfaces...
==> server1: Mounting shared folders...
    server1: /vagrant => /Users/michael/Documents/projects/packt-vagrant-book
==> server2: Importing base box 'hashicorp/precise64'...
==> server2: Matching MAC address for NAT networking...
==> server2: Checking if box 'hashicorp/precise64' is up to date...
==> server2: Setting the name of the VM: packt-vagrant-book_server2_1414969743105_97374
==> server2: Fixed port collision for 22 => 2222. Now on port 2200.
==> server2: Clearing any previously set network interfaces...
==> server2: Preparing network interfaces based on configuration...
    server2: Adapter 1: nat
    server2: Adapter 2: hostonly
==> server2: Forwarding ports...
    server2: 22 => 2200 (adapter 1)
==> server2: Booting VM...
==> server2: Waiting for machine to boot. This may take a few minutes...
    server2: SSH address: 127.0.0.1:2200
    server2: SSH username: vagrant
    server2: SSH auth method: private key
    server2: Warning: Connection timeout. Retrying...
==> server2: Machine booted and ready!
==> server2: Checking for guest additions in VM...
    server2: The guest additions on this VM do not match the installed version of
    server2: VirtualBox! In most cases this is fine, but in rare cases it can
    server2: prevent things such as shared folders from working properly. If you see
    server2: shared folder errors, please make sure the guest additions within the
```

As shown in the preceding screenshot, Vagrant maps the SSH port on the virtual machine designated **server1** to port **2222** on the host machine, and the SSH port of the machine designated **server2** to the port **2200**.

This gives us the opportunity of simply using the standard SSH command from a terminal (or the likes of PuTTY on a Windows machine), to connect to localhost with the port number that Vagrant assigns to each machine.

To connect to the machine that is mapped to port `2200`, we simply run the `ssh vagrant@localhost -p2200` command. The `-p2200` option tells the command to use a nonstandard port, and specifies the port we wish to use, in this case `2200`.

Alternatively, we can use the `vagrant ssh` command to connect to the virtual machines. The difference is that in a multivirtual machine environment, we must also provide the name of the virtual machine. For example, `vagrant ssh server1`. This is the most common usage of connecting to a machine, rather than directly connecting to the virtual machine via its IP address.

```
Michaels-MBP:packt-vagrant-book michael$ vagrant ssh server1
Welcome to Ubuntu 12.04 LTS (GNU/Linux 3.2.0-23-generic x86_64)

 * Documentation:  https://help.ubuntu.com/
New release '14.04.1 LTS' available.
Run 'do-release-upgrade' to upgrade to it.

Welcome to your Vagrant-built virtual machine.
Last login: Sun Nov  2 23:16:51 2014 from 10.0.2.2
vagrant@precise64:~$
```

Networking the multiple virtual machines

In a single virtual machine project, the IP address of the virtual machine isn't that important. In a multivirtual machine project, however, it is more likely that we want the two machines to communicate with one another directly; in order to do this, we need to be aware of their IP addresses, or we need to forward nonconflicting ports to the localhost instead. As we want to have our Vagrant projects distributed to our team members, and some of these team members may be within the same office, we need to:

- Predefine the IP address so that any of our projects code that needs to communicate with the other virtual machine can do so, without the other team members needing to change configurations
- Ensure that the virtual machines are running on a private network only that are attached to the machine of the user running it; this will prevent the IP address conflicts within the network

Working with Multiple Machines

In order to do this, we simply use the networking options, which we learned in *Chapter 2, Managing Vagrant Boxes and Projects*. Because we want the virtual machines to run in a private network, it makes sense to use a range of private IP addresses, which are different to your own network. For example, my network range is 192.168.1.xxx, so I will use the range 10.11.1.xxx for my virtual machine network (the IP address ranges are a subset of the range of addresses preassigned for internal networks), as shown in the following code:

```ruby
# -*- mode: ruby -*-
# vi: set ft=ruby :

VAGRANTFILE_API_VERSION = "2"

Vagrant.configure(VAGRANTFILE_API_VERSION) do |config|

  config.vm.define :server1 do |server1|
    server1.vm.box = "hashicorp/precise64"
    server1.vm.network "private_network", ip: "10.11.1.100"
  end

  config.vm.define :server2 do |server2|
    server2.vm.box = "hashicorp/precise64"
    server2.vm.network :private_network, ip: "10.11.1.101"
  end

end
```

Let's test this out and test whether we can connect from one machine to the other:

1. Power up the project (vagrant up).
2. Connect to server1 (vagrant ssh server1).
3. Ping server2 from server1 (ping 10.11.1.101).

The output shows that we are able to communicate over the network from `server1` to `server2` as follows:

```
Michaels-MBP:packt-vagrant-book michael$ vagrant ssh server1
Welcome to Ubuntu 12.04 LTS (GNU/Linux 3.2.0-23-generic x86_64)

 * Documentation:  https://help.ubuntu.com/
New release '14.04.1 LTS' available.
Run 'do-release-upgrade' to upgrade to it.

Welcome to your Vagrant-built virtual machine.
Last login: Fri Sep 14 06:23:18 2012 from 10.0.2.2
vagrant@precise64:~$ ping 10.11.1.101
PING 10.11.1.101 (10.11.1.101) 56(84) bytes of data.
64 bytes from 10.11.1.101: icmp_req=1 ttl=64 time=1.48 ms
64 bytes from 10.11.1.101: icmp_req=2 ttl=64 time=0.936 ms
64 bytes from 10.11.1.101: icmp_req=3 ttl=64 time=0.793 ms
^C
--- 10.11.1.101 ping statistics ---
3 packets transmitted, 3 received, 0% packet loss, time 2004ms
rtt min/avg/max/mdev = 0.793/1.072/1.487/0.299 ms
vagrant@precise64:~$
```

Provisioning the machines separately

As the virtual machines in our projects are going to be used for different purposes, we need to use different provisioning for the machines, so they both have only the software and configurations needed to do their job.

We take the provisioning code, which we learned in *Chapter 3*, *Provisioning with Puppet*, and *Chapter 6*, *Provisioning Vagrant Machines with Puppet, Ansible, and Chef*, and we place the relevant code within the virtual machine's subconfiguration. There are some key changes that we need to make:

- The opening line of the provision code must reference the server name of the virtual machine it relates to
- For Puppet, we should use a different manifest file for the two virtual machines
- For Chef, we will apply different roles to the different machines

Working with Multiple Machines

The following code provisions both the machines using Puppet. They both rely on the same set of Puppet modules, the same path that points to the manifests folder, however, they both use different manifests to set up the projects (alternatively, we can configure the machines and identify them as nodes to a Puppet master to retrieve the appropriate configuration):

```ruby
# -*- mode: ruby -*-
# vi: set ft=ruby :

VAGRANTFILE_API_VERSION = "2"

Vagrant.configure(VAGRANTFILE_API_VERSION) do |config|

  config.vm.define :server1 do |server1|
    server1.vm.box = "hashicorp/precise64"
    server1.vm.network "private_network", ip: "10.11.1.100"

    server1.vm.provision :puppet do |puppet|
      puppet.manifests_path = "provision/puppet/manifests"
      puppet.manifest_file  = "server1.pp"
      puppet.module_path = "provision/puppet/modules"
    end

  end

  config.vm.define :server2 do |server2|
    server2.vm.box = "hashicorp/precise64"
    server2.vm.network :private_network, ip: "10.11.1.101"

    server2.vm.provision :puppet do |puppet|
      puppet.manifests_path = "provision/puppet/manifests"
      puppet.manifest_file  = "server2.pp"
      puppet.module_path = "provision/puppet/modules"
    end

  end

end
```

Within the provisions for each machine, we would need to ensure that we allow both the machines to communicate with one another. For example, by default, a MySQL Server won't accept connections from a remote server, so we would need to modify (or replace) the configuration file with one that allows this, or we would need to use a Puppet module or Chef cookbook that allows us to modify this configuration value.

> You should check the documentation for any software you are communicating with over the network to see how it needs to be configured. With MySQL, you need to edit the my.cnf file, and set the bind address to 0.0.0.0.

Destroying a multimachine project

If we want to completely remove the virtual machines for our project from our host machine, we can use the vagrant destroy command, as with normal projects. The difference being that Vagrant will ask us to confirm the removal of each machine within the project:

```
Michaels-MacBook-Pro:mutlimachine michael$ vagrant destroy
Are you sure you want to destroy the 'database' VM? [y/N] y
[database] Forcing shutdown of VM...
[database] Destroying VM and associated drives...
Are you sure you want to destroy the 'webserver' VM? [y/N] y
[webserver] Forcing shutdown of VM...
[webserver] Destroying VM and associated drives...
```

Summary

In this chapter, we set up a Vagrant project that uses multiple virtual machines. During the course of this chapter, we learned how to create multiple virtual machines within a single project. In order to achieve this, we also looked at how to assign specific names to these individual machines, how to connect to the individual machines over SSH (as previously vagrant ssh would take us to just a single machine), and how to configure the individual machines, specifying IP addresses, base boxes, and different provisioning options for them.

Now, we learned the vast majority of Vagrant's functionality and how to use it within different project scenarios. In the next chapter, we will take a look at how to build our own custom base box to use with our projects, configuring a blank operating system installation into a compatible base image.

8
Creating Your Own Box

So far, we have used Vagrant with the freely available base boxes. There are also many other existing base Vagrant boxes out there. In *Chapter 9*, *HashiCorp Atlas*, we will talk about how we can discover and distribute base boxes. When we discussed Vagrant boxes initially in *Chapter 1*, *Getting Started with Vagrant*, and *Chapter 2*, *Managing Vagrant Boxes and Projects*, we learned about how we can export a Vagrant environment into a new base box.

Creating a new base box involves us either taking an existing box, making changes to it, and exporting it, or creating a new virtual machine entirely, installing the operating system and building up a base box for export. In this chapter, we will take a look at how we can take a Linux installation disk and turn it into a working Vagrant base box, which we can further customize as much as we like.

In this chapter, you will learn about the following topics:

- How to create a new VirtualBox machine, suitably configured for Vagrant
- How to install the VirtualBox Guest Additions
- How to set up the Linux installation to let Vagrant log in
- How to install Puppet
- How to install Chef
- How to clean up the box
- How to export the VM into a base box

Getting started

In order to create a new base box, we need to download a copy of the operating system we want to use (we will use Ubuntu Server Version 13.04 64-bit from `http://releases.ubuntu.com/raring/`). We then need to use VirtualBox to create a virtual machine, powered by the operating system we have downloaded. Next, we need to configure the virtual machine for Vagrant. Finally, we need to export the virtual machine into a Vagrant base box.

> You can also use other distributions of Linux or even Windows if you wish. Specifics will vary with the operating system used, so you will need to consult the relevant documentation.

The requirements for a new base box are detailed on the Vagrant website (`https://docs.vagrantup.com/v2/boxes/base.html`).

Preparing the VirtualBox machine

In order to create the virtual machine with VirtualBox, we need to open the VirtualBox and click on the **New** button in the upper-left corner of the VirtualBox to start the process:

Let's name the machine `vagrant-ubuntu-raring`. This is the format recommended by Vagrant. Select **Linux** in the **Type** dropdown and **Version** as **Ubuntu (64 bit)**:

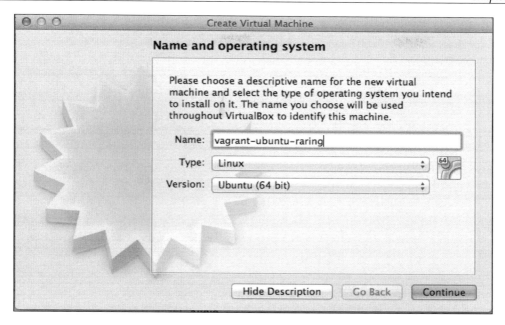

Vagrant recommends setting a memory allocation of **360 MB**. This is typically sufficient for a base installation, and users can override this within their Vagrantfile if they need more resources:

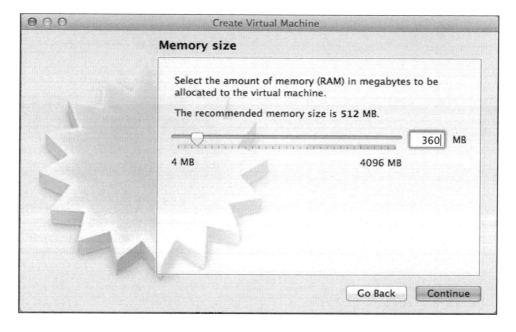

Creating Your Own Box

We need our virtual machine to have some storage allocation, so let's select **Create a virtual hard drive now**:

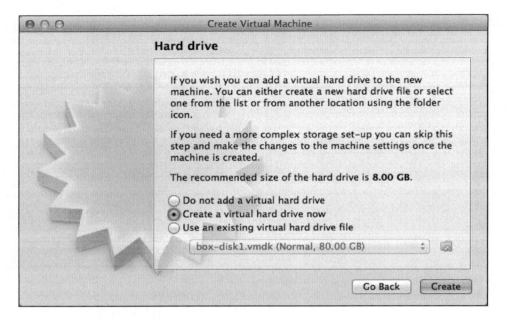

We need to select **VMDK (Virtual Machine Disk)** as the disk type:

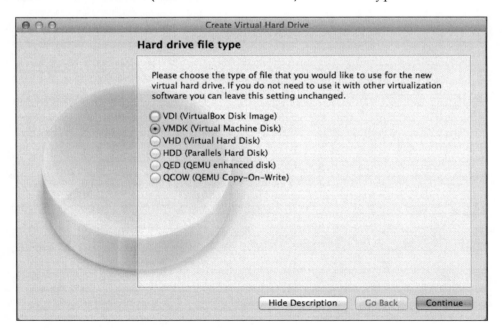

We need to create a drive, which is dynamically allocated:

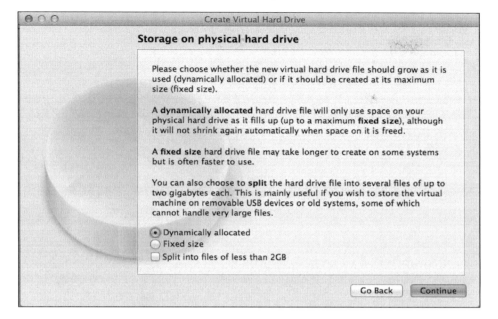

Let's give the drive a maximum limit of **40.00 GB**; the Vagrant documentation suggests that this is typically sufficient for many projects:

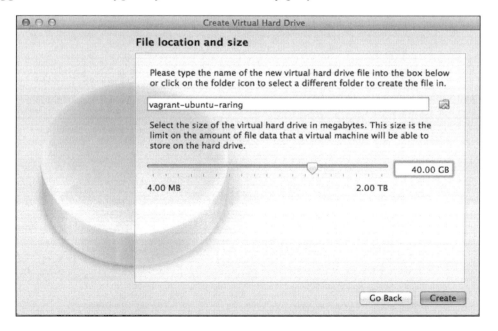

Creating Your Own Box

Clicking on **Create** will then save the virtual machine within VirtualBox. We need to make some additional configuration changes, which are not a part of the creation wizard, so let's click on the VM on the left-hand side of the screen, and then click on the **Settings** button:

The first additional change is **Audio**, so let's turn this off:

We need to ensure that the network adapter configured within VirtualBox is enabled and uses **NAT**. Without this, Vagrant won't work:

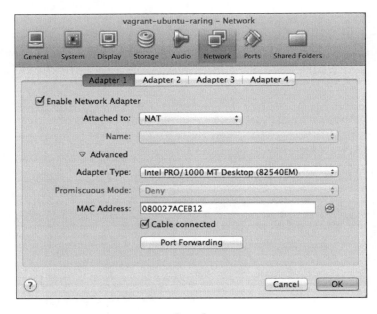

Finally, let's turn off USB support, as this is generally not required:

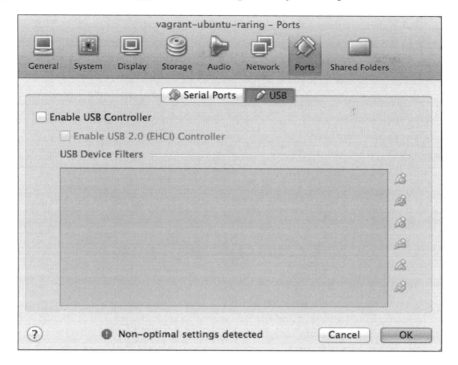

Now we need to switch on the virtual machine. When it powers on, it asks us to select a startup disk, which contains the operating system we wish to install. Clicking on the folder icon on this screen lets us select a custom file; in our case, this will be our `ubuntu-13.04-server-amd64.iso` file.

The virtual machine will then boot from the image file and take us to the installation process. We should follow this process to set up the machine.

There are some specific values for some things that Vagrant expects, so wherever appropriate we should ensure that we set them as follows:

- By convention, the operating system's hostname should be of the `vagrant-operating-system-name` format, for example, `vagrant-ubuntu-raring`
- The domain is `vagrantup.com`
- The root password is `vagrant`
- The main account username is `vagrant`
- The main account password is `vagrant`

Creating Your Own Box

In most other cases, the default options will be fine, as we will configure other aspects later. When prompted as to any packages to install by default, we should select to install **openssh-server**.

VirtualBox Guest Additions

First, let's log in to our new virtual machine within VirtualBox. Once logged in, at the terminal, we should run `apt-get update` to update our package manager.

Vagrant has a set of tools called Guest Additions that provide some key integration points between the virtual machine and VirtualBox; this includes support for shared folders and networking integration.

To install these tools, once the VM is running, we should click on the **Devices** menu within Virtual Box and click on **Install Guest Additions... (Host+D)**:

This simply boots a virtual CD within the virtual machine; we still need to actually install the Guest Additions, as follows:

1. The first step is to install a prerequisite, which are the Linux headers:
   `sudo apt-get install linux-headers-$(uname -r) build-essential`

2. Next, we will mount the virtual CD, which VirtualBox has loaded up into a folder within the VM:
   `sudo mount /dev/cdrom /media/cdrom`

3. Finally, we will run the installation command:
   `sudo sh /media/cdrom/VBoxLinuxAdditions.run`

Vagrant authentication

Vagrant communicates with base boxes over SSH. Vagrant itself has a private key, for which we need to install the corresponding public key into the virtual machine. Vagrant expects a specific user with a predefined password to also be within the machine, and the user needs to be configured so that it isn't prompted for the password when attempting to perform actions that require elevated privileges (sudo).

Vagrant user and admin group

Provided we created the Vagrant user during the installation process (as per the main account user and password mentioned earlier), we then need to create an `admin` group and add the Vagrant user to this group.

First, we need to create the group:

```
Sudo groupadd admin
```

To add the Vagrant user to this group, run the following command:

```
Sudo usermod -a -G admin vagrant
```

The sudoers file

In order to stop the virtual machine asking for the user's password when running elevated actions, we need to modify the `sudoers` file. This is a file that tells the operating system which users can perform elevated actions and the settings around them. More information can be found at https://help.ubuntu.com/community/Sudoers. We need to add a configuration line to this file, which tells the operating system not to prompt for the password. Because the file is very important, and an incorrect configuration would break the operating system, there is a program built into Ubuntu, which won't save if the file is not edited correctly.

First, let's run this program:

```
visudo
```

At the bottom of the file, let's add this line to prevent the operating system from prompting for the password:

```
%admin ALL=(ALL) NOPASSWD: ALL
```

Another requirement of Vagrant is that we add the following line near the top of the file:

```
Defaults env_keep="SSH_AUTH_SOCK"
```

Creating Your Own Box

We also need to disable `requiretty` in the `sudoers` file by commenting out the appropriate line as follows:

```
#Default requiretty
```

 `requiretty` is an option that requires users to have a physical connection to a server in order to run the `sudo` commands.

Insecure public/private key pair

The insecure public and private key pair is publicly available at `https://github.com/mitchellh/vagrant/tree/master/keys/`.

 An upcoming version of Vagrant will change how Vagrant works with these insecure keys. When detected, they will be replaced with new keys for your machine; however, at time of writing, this has not yet been released.

We need to copy the contents of the public key and paste it into the `authorized_hosts` file. Provided we are logged in as the Vagrant user, we can run the following command to let us edit this file:

`nano ~/.ssh/authorized_hosts`

If the `.ssh` folder does not already exist, we first need to create it using the `mkdir` command. Alternatively, we can download the file contents and put it straight into the `authorized_hosts` file:

```
wget
  https://raw.github.com/mitchellh/vagrant/master/keys/
    vagrant.pub -O ~/.ssh/authorized_hosts
```

 The `.ssh` directory needs to have permissions of `0700`, and the `authorized_hosts` file needs to have permissions of `0644` (`chmod 0644 ~/.ssh/authorized_keys`).

Provisioners

Because Vagrant provides support for provisioners, we should install these into the virtual machine so that Vagrant can tell them to provision our environments.

Installing Puppet

Puppet is installed using the built-in package manager:

```
sudo apt-get install puppet
```

> The version of Puppet in the various operating system repositories may be slightly dated. Puppet can also be installed manually or via the repository site provided by Puppet Labs. More information is available on the Puppet labs website at http://docs.puppetlabs.com/guides/installation.html.

Installing Chef

As per the Chef documentation at https://www.chef.io/download-chef-client/, we can get a single command to install Chef for us:

```
curl -L https://www.chef.io/chef/install.sh | sudo bash
```

Cleaning up the VM

Before we package up the virtual machine into a Vagrant base box, let's clean up some of the files we used. We made use of the tmp folder, so let's empty this. We should also clean up our package manager's cache, as this uses additional space when the base box is packaged:

```
rm -rf /tmp/*
sudo apt-get clean
```

Export

Finally, we use Vagrant's package subcommand on the host machine (not the guest) to package up the box:

```
vagrant package --base vagrant-ubuntu-raring
```

The complete details of the package subcommand are available on the Vagrant website (http://docs.vagrantup.com/v2/cli/package.html).

Summary

In this chapter, we learned how to create, a base box for our Vagrant projects from scratch. This can be used to create base boxes from operating systems, which don't necessarily have boxes available to download.

Now, we know how to create, manage, distribute, and even build development environments from scratch for our projects!

Next, we will take a look at Vagrant Cloud, which lets us search for and discover different base boxes as well as letting us distribute our own box—either to the public or to a private team. Vagrant Cloud also has the functionality to allow us to share our Vagrant development environment with others—be that to demonstrate the functionality we have built on a Vagrant-supported project, or to provide SSH access to a team member who can help us with support issues.

9
HashiCorp Atlas

HashiCorp Atlas (https://atlas.hashicorp.com), formerly Vagrant Cloud, is a suite of online services provided by HashiCorp (the commercial company behind Vagrant), which adds additional capabilities to Vagrant and brings together many of their open source components. Primarily, Atlas supports two features:

- **Vagrant Share**: The ability to share access to your Vagrant environment and to allow others to remotely connect to it
- **Vagrant box discovery and sharing**: The ability to share Vagrant boxes with others, hosting the metadata for boxes, their versions, and facilitating box updates

These features are available free of charge, though paying customers can gain access to additional functionality, including the following:

- Custom and static domain names for Vagrant Share
- Private boxes that can be shared with specific teams privately
- Box hosting: Vagrant Cloud will actually store the box file on their platform as well as the metadata
- Support for Windows and Mac Vagrant boxes
- Granular support for user access controls

In this chapter, you will learn about the following topics:

- How to discover and use boxes provided on Atlas
- How to distribute your own boxes on Atlas
- How to allow others to connect to your Vagrant machine through Atlas
- How to share your Vagrant machine through Atlas

Discovering boxes

The Atlas website contains a directory of public boxes for Vagrant (https://atlas.hashicorp.com/boxes/search). Within this directory, we can search for the specific operating system or distribution version that we are interested in:

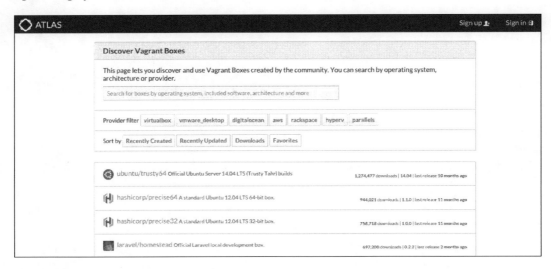

For each result, we can see the box name, which is formatted as the name of the distributor followed by a slash, followed by the name or distribution name. In the following case, we have the Ubuntu 12.04 LTS release that HashiCorp has provided (named **hashicorp/precise64**):

If we click in a box, we can see which *providers* the box supports. In this case, we can use the box with **VirtualBox**, **VMware Fusion**, and **Hyper-V**. It is important to use boxes that support the provider we are using—not all boxes support all providers.

Installing new boxes

To install a public box, we use the vagrant box add command, and pass the name of the box:

```
vagrant box add hashicorp/precise64
```

The name of the box can either be a URL or file path to an existing box file (for example, if we have one stored on our network that we wish to use) or an Atlas box name, like in the preceding command.

Updating existing boxes

One of the key benefits of using Atlas for box discovery is that changes and versions of these boxes can be managed. If a particular box contains a bug or security vulnerability, distributors may update their boxes to fix these issues, or contain new functionality. This can be useful, as it saves us the need to update our provisioning configuration to make these updates.

When in a Vagrant projects folder, we can run the following command to check for updates for the projects box and update it:

`vagrant box update`

This will download the new box; however, we won't see the effect of the new box unless we destroy our Vagrant machine and rebuild it from the updated box.

If we want to update a specific box, as opposed to the one that is tied to the project we are in, we can use the box flag to provide the name of the box we want to update:

`vagrant box update --box the-box/name`

Checking for outdated boxes

We can quickly check to see whether any of the boxes we installed are out of date, by running the following command:

`vagrant box outdated --global`

If we omit the `global` flag, then the command is only within the context of the current Vagrant project with the flag it relates to all boxes installed:

```
Michaels-MBP:packt-vagrant-temp michael$ vagrant box outdated --global
* 'ubuntu/trusty64' (v14.04) is up to date
* 'quantal64_roderik' wasn't added from a catalog, no version information
* 'quantal64' wasn't added from a catalog, no version information
* 'precise64' wasn't added from a catalog, no version information
* 'laravel/homestead' is outdated! Current: 0.1.9. Latest: 0.2.0
* 'hashicorp/precise64' (v1.1.0) is up to date
Michaels-MBP:packt-vagrant-temp michael$
```

HashiCorp Atlas

Distributing boxes

To distribute boxes with Atlas, we need to create an account and log in to the Atlas website (https://atlas.hashicorp.com/account/new). The username that we select when registering is used as the prefix for boxes we distribute—unless, of course, we go onto a paid plan, which has organizational support, or we collaborate with others on a box. Once logged in, we need to click on the **Create Box** link to go to the box creation form (https://atlas.hashicorp.com/boxes/new).

On this page, we need to provide a name and description for our box. As we are on the free plan, we cannot make this a private box, so it will be made public:

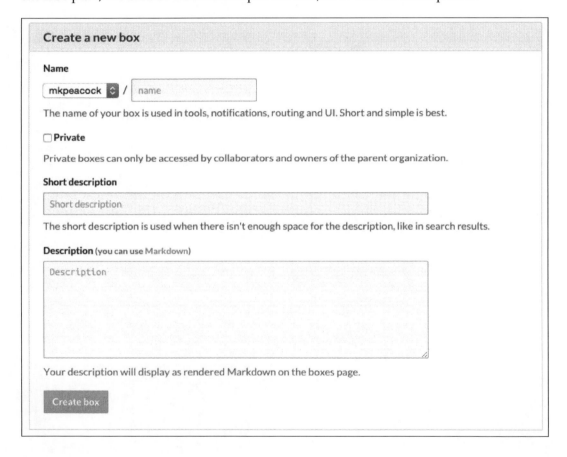

As the boxes distributed through Atlas can be versioned, to let us roll out new updates to users of the box, we need to create an initial version for the box, along with a description of what the version contains:

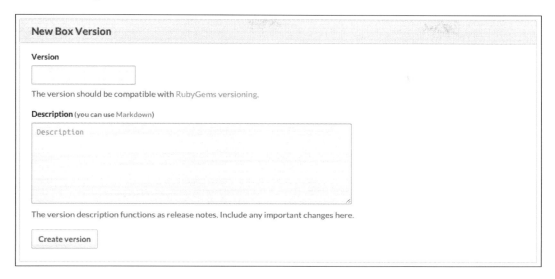

Next, we need to click on **Create new provider** to add a new provider that is supported by this version of the box:

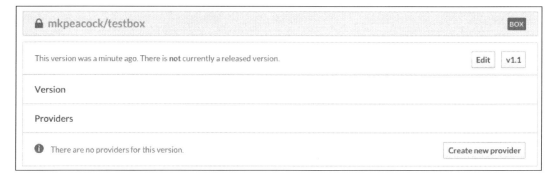

Finally, we specify the provider, and provide a URL to where the box can be downloaded. With the free version of Atlas, we need to provide a link to the box, as there is no storage allowance for Vagrant Cloud to host the file for us:

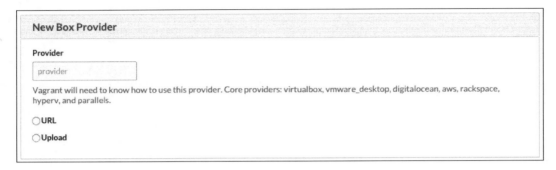

Once a box has been created and published, it can be discovered and installed, as we discussed in the *Discovering boxes* section, by the public, or by us using the name of the box in our Vagrantfile, for example, `mkpeacock/testbox`.

Sharing and connecting with Atlas

With Atlas, there are three new Vagrant commands at our disposal, which are as follows:

- `vagrant connect`
- `vagrant share`
- `vagrant login`

Logging Vagrant into Vagrant Cloud

In order to share our Vagrant environment, we need to connect our Vagrant installation to our Vagrant Cloud account. We can check to see whether this is already the case by running the following command:

```
vagrant login --check
```

This will check to see whether we are already logged in:

```
Michaels-MBP:packt-vagrant-temp michael$ vagrant login --check
You aren't logged in! Run `vagrant login` to log in.
```

As we are not logged in, we need to run `vagrant login` in order to log in. First, we are prompted for our username or e-mail address from Atlas, and then for our password:

```
Michaels-MBP:packt-vagrant-temp michael$ vagrant login
In a moment we'll ask for your username and password to Vagrant Cloud.
After authenticating, we will store an access token locally. Your
login details will be transmitted over a secure connection, and are
never stored on disk locally.

If you don't have a Vagrant Cloud account, sign up at vagrantcloud.com

Username or Email: mkpeacock@gmail.com
Password (will be hidden):
You're now logged in!
Michaels-MBP:packt-vagrant-temp michael$
```

Once logged in, we can use the `logout` flag to log out of Atlas:

`vagrant login --logout`

```
Michaels-MBP:packt-vagrant-temp michael$ vagrant login --logout
You are logged out.
```

Sharing a Vagrant virtual machine over HTTP(S)

In order to share the web interface with a Vagrant virtual machine, the virtual machine must either have its own IP address on our local network or an HTTP(S) port forwarded from the guest to the host machine. Vagrant requires this so that your host machine can connect to the relevant port on your virtual machine.

Provided we have either given the virtual machine its own network address or forward a port to a recognizable HTTP(S) port, then we can run the `vagrant share` command to create a public URL for this machine. We can also specify the HTTP and HTTPS ports that we are using on the virtual machine if Vagrant doesn't detect them with the `--http` and `--https` flags:

```
Michaels-MBP:packt-vagrant-temp michael$ vagrant share
==> default: Detecting network information for machine...
    default: Local machine address: 192.168.33.10
    default: Local HTTP port: 80
    default: Local HTTPS port: disabled
==> default: Checking authentication and authorization...
==> default: Creating Vagrant Share session...
    default: Share will be at: profound-cony-6698
==> default: Your Vagrant Share is running! Name: profound-cony-6698
==> default: URL: http://profound-cony-6698.vagrantshare.com
```

After running `vagrant share`, Vagrant will generate a name and URL to access the share from. As we are on a free plan, we cannot customize or reserve URLs. Our terminal session is now locked to run this sharing session, so we need to leave this running. If we visit the URL in a browser, we should be able to see whatever web service we are running on our virtual machine:

To stop sharing, we need to close the terminal or stop the `vagrant share` command from running:

```
^CExiting due to interrupt.
Michaels-MBP:packt-vagrant-temp michael$
```

Sharing and connecting to a Vagrant virtual machine

By default, `vagrant share` only shares HTTP(S) traffic. We can, however, pass the `--ssh` flag to also share SSH access that will allow other Vagrant users to connect to the machine:

`vagrant share --ssh`

After running this command, we will be prompted to provide and confirm a password to be used to encrypt the SSH key so that the users are required to provide a password when they connect. If required, this can be omitted with the `--ssh-no-password` flag instead of `--ssh`. We can also make a single use SSH connection with `--ssh-once`, as shown in the following screenshot:

```
Michaels-MBP:packt-vagrant-temp michael$ vagrant share --ssh
==> default: Detecting network information for machine...
    default: Local machine address: 192.168.33.10
    default: Local HTTP port: 80
    default: Local HTTPS port: disabled
    default: SSH Port: 22
==> default: Generating new SSH key...
    default: Please enter a password to encrypt the key:
    default: Repeat the password to confirm:
    default: Inserting generated SSH key into machine...
==> default: Checking authentication and authorization...
==> default: Creating Vagrant Share session...
    default: Share will be at: difficult-elephant-4464
    default: Your Vagrant Share is running! Name: difficult-elephant-4464
    default: URL: http://difficult-elephant-4464.vagrantshare.com
    default:
    default: You're sharing with SSH access. This means that another user
    default: simply has to run `vagrant connect --ssh difficult-elephant-4464`
    default: to SSH to your Vagrant machine.
    default:
    default: Because you encrypted your SSH private key with a password,
    default: the other user will be prompted for this password when they
    default: run `vagrant connect --ssh`. Please share this password with them
    default: in some secure way.
```

As with a regular `share` command, we get a URL and a name. We can prevent HTTP(S) from being shared by passing the `--disable-http` flag.

Once the sharing process is running, we can provide the name and password to whomever we want to be able to connect to the machine. They simply run the `vagrant connect --ssh difficult-elephant-4464` command (where the last parameter is the name of the connection generated by Atlas) to start a connection with the machine, and provide the password when prompted:

```
Michaels-MacBook-Pro-2:packt-vagrant-temp michael$ vagrant connect --ssh difficult-elephant-4464
Loading share 'difficult-elephant-4464'...
The SSH key to connect to this share is encrypted. You will require
the password entered when creating to share to decrypt it. Verify you
access to this password before continuing.

Press enter to continue, or Ctrl-C to exit now.
Password for the private key:
Executing SSH...
Welcome to Ubuntu 14.04 LTS (GNU/Linux 3.13.0-24-generic x86_64)

 * Documentation:  https://help.ubuntu.com/

  System information as of Thu Nov 13 18:58:33 UTC 2014

  System load:  0.0               Processes:           78
  Usage of /:   2.7% of 39.34GB   Users logged in:     0
  Memory usage: 26%               IP address for eth0: 10.0.2.15
  Swap usage:   0%                IP address for eth1: 192.168.33.10

  Graph this data and manage this system at:
    https://landscape.canonical.com/

  Get cloud support with Ubuntu Advantage Cloud Guest:
    http://www.ubuntu.com/business/services/cloud
```

The user is then logged into the Vagrant machine!

Summary

In this chapter, we learned about the extra functionality offered by the Vagrant Cloud service.

We discovered how to find third-party Vagrant boxes for use with our projects, how to check for updates for boxes that use Atlas, and how to distribute our own base boxes through Atlas. Finally, we looked at authenticating with Atlas to share our Vagrant environment with our colleagues.

Now that we know more about the functionality offered by Vagrant, we can use it effectively in our projects!

A Sample LEMP Stack

Now that we have a good knowledge of using Vagrant to manage software development projects and how to use the Puppet provisioning tool, let's take a look at how to use these tools to build a **Linux, Nginx, MySQL, and PHP (LEMP)** development environment with Vagrant.

In this appendix, you will learn the following topics:

- How to update the package manager
- How to create a LEMP-based development environment in Vagrant, including the following:
    - How to install the Nginx web server
    - How to customize the Nginx configuration file
    - How to install PHP
    - How to install and configure MySQL
    - How to install e-mail sending services

With the exception of MySQL, we will create simple Puppet modules to install and manage the software required. For MySQL, we will use the official Puppet module from Puppet Labs; this module makes it very easy for us to install and configure all aspects of MySQL.

Creating the Vagrant project

First, we want to create a new project, so let's create a new folder called `lemp-stack` and initialize a new `ubuntu/trusty64` Vagrant project within it by executing the following commands:

```
mkdir lemp-stack
cd lemp-stack
vagrant init ubuntu/trusty64 ub
```

The easiest way for us to pull in the MySQL Puppet module is to simply add it as a `git` submodule to our project. In order to add a `git` submodule, our project needs to be a `git` repository, so let's initialize it as a `git` repository now to save time later:

`git init`

To make the virtual machine reflective of a real-world production server, instead of forwarding the web server port on the virtual machine to another port on our host machine, we will instead network the virtual machine. This means that we would be able to access the web server via port `80` (which is typical on a production web server) by connecting directly to the virtual machine.

In order to ensure a fixed IP address to which we can allocate a hostname on our network, we need to uncomment the following line from our Vagrantfile by removing the # from the start of the line:

```
# config.vm.network "private_network", ip: "192.168.33.10"
```

The IP address can be changed depending on the needs of our project.

As this is a sample LEMP stack designed for web-based projects, let's configure our projects directory to a relevant web folder on the virtual machine:

```
config.vm.synced_folder ".", "/var/www/project", type: "nfs"
```

We will still need to configure our web server to point to this folder; however, it is more appropriate than the default mapping location of `/vagrant`.

Before we run our Puppet provisioner to install our LEMP stack, we should instruct Vagrant to run the `apt-get update` command on the virtual machine. Without this, it isn't always possible to install new packages. So, let's add the following line to our Vagrant file within the |config| block:

```
config.vm.provision "shell", inline: "apt-get update"
```

As we will put our Puppet modules and manifests in a `provision` folder, we need to configure Vagrant to use the correct folders for our Puppet manifests and modules as well as the default manifest file. Adding the following code to our Vagrantfile will do this for us:

```
config.vm.provision :puppet do |puppet|
    puppet.manifests_path = "provision/manifests"
    puppet.module_path    = "provision/modules"
    puppet.manifest_file  = "vagrant.pp"
end
```

Creating the Puppet manifests

Let's start by creating some folders for our Puppet modules and manifests by executing the following commands:

`mkdir provision`

`cd provision`

`mkdir modules`

`mkdir manifests`

For each of the modules we want to create, we need to create a folder within the `provision/modules` folder for the module. Within this folder, we need to create a `manifests` folder, and within this, our Puppet manifest file, `init.pp`. Structurally, this looks something like the following:

```
|-- provision
|    |-- manifests
|    |    `-- vagrant.pp
|    `-- modules
|         |-- our module
|              |-- manifests
|                   `-- init.pp
`-- Vagrantfile
```

Installing Nginx

Let's take a look at what is involved to install Nginx through a module and manifest file `provision/modules/nginx/manifests/init.pp`. First, we define our class, passing in a variable so that we can change the configuration file we use for Nginx (useful for using the same module for different projects or different environments such as staging and production environments), then we need to ensure that the `nginx` package is installed:

```
class nginx ($file = 'default') {

  package {"nginx":
    ensure => present
  }
```

 Note that we have not closed the curly bracket for the `nginx` class. That is because this is just the first snippet of the file; we will close it at the end.

A Sample LEMP Stack

Because we want to change our default Nginx configuration file, we should update the contents of the Nginx configuration file with one of our own (this will need to be placed in the `provision/modules/nginx/files` folder; unless the `file` parameter is passed to the class, the file `default` will be used):

```
file { '/etc/nginx/sites-available/default':
    source => "puppet:///modules/nginx/${file}",
    owner => 'root',
    group => 'root',
    notify => Service['nginx'],
    require => Package['nginx']
}
```

Finally, we need to ensure that the `nginx` service is actually running once it has been installed:

```
service { "nginx":
    ensure => running,
    require => Package["nginx"]
  }
}
```

This completes the manifest. We do still, however, need to create a default configuration file for Nginx, which is saved as `provision/modules/nginx/files/default`. This will be used unless we pass a `file` parameter to the `nginx` class when using the module. The sample file here is a basic configuration file, pointing to the `public` folder within our `synced` folder. The server name of `lemp-stack.local` means that Nginx will listen for requests on that hostname and will serve content from our projects folder:

```
server {
    listen    80;

    root /var/www/project/public;
    index index.php index.html index.htm;

    server_name lemp-stack.local;

    location / {
        try_files $uri $uri/ /index.php?$query_string;
    }

    location ~ \.php$ {
        try_files $uri =404;
        fastcgi_split_path_info ^(.+\.php)(/.+)$;
```

```
            #fastcgi_pass 127.0.0.1:9000;
            fastcgi_param SERVER_NAME $host;
            fastcgi_pass unix:/var/run/php5-fpm.sock;
            fastcgi_index index.php;
            fastcgi_intercept_errors on;
            include fastcgi_params;
        }

        location ~ /\.ht {
            deny all;
        }

        location ~* \.(jpg|jpeg|gif|css|png|js|ico|html)$ {
            access_log off;
            expires max;
        }

        location ~* \.svgz {
            add_header Content-Encoding "gzip";
        }
    }
```

> Because this configuration file listens for requests on `lemp-stack.local`, we need to add a record to the `hosts` file on our host machine, which will redirect traffic from `lemp-stack.local` to the IP address of our virtual machine.

Installing PHP

To install PHP, we need to install a range of related packages, including the Nginx PHP module. This would be in the file `provision/modules/php/manifests/init.pp`.

On more recent (within the past few years) Linux and PHP installations, PHP uses a handler called `php-fpm` as a bridge between PHP and the web server being used. This means that when new PHP modules are installed or PHP configurations are changed, we need to restart the `php-fpm` service for these changes to take effect, whereas in the past, it was often the web servers that needed to be restarted or reloaded.

A Sample LEMP Stack

To make our simple PHP Puppet module flexible, we need to install the `php5-fpm` package and restart it when other modules are installed, but only when we use Nginx on our server. To achieve this, we can use a `class` parameter, which defaults to `true`. This lets us use the same module in servers that don't have a web server, and where we don't want to have the overhead of the FPM service, such as a server that runs background jobs or processing:

```
class php ($nginx = true) {
```

If the `nginx` parameter is `true`, then we need to install `php5-fpm`. Since this package is only installed when the flag is set to `true`, we cannot have PHP and its modules requiring or notifying the `php-fpm` package, as it may not be installed; so instead we need to have the `php5-fpm` package subscribe to these packages:

```
    if ($nginx) {
        package { "php5-fpm":
          ensure => present,
          subscribe => [Package['php5-dev'], Package['php5-curl'],
Package['php5-gd'], Package['php5-imagick'], Package['php5-mcrypt'],
Package['php5-mhash'], Package['php5-pspell'], Package['php5-json'],
Package['php5-xmlrpc'], Package['php5-xsl'], Package['php5-mysql']]
        }
    }
```

The rest of the manifest can then simply be the installation of the various PHP modules that are required for a typical LEMP setup:

```
    package { "php5-dev":
        ensure => present
    }

    package { "php5-curl":
        ensure => present
    }

    package { "php5-gd":
        ensure => present
    }

    package { "php5-imagick":
        ensure => present
    }

    package { "php5-mcrypt":
```

```
        ensure => present
    }

    package { "php5-mhash":
        ensure => present
    }

    package { "php5-pspell":
        ensure => present
    }

    package { "php5-xmlrpc":
        ensure => present
    }

    package { "php5-xsl":
        ensure => present
    }

    package { "php5-cli":
        ensure => present
    }

    package { "php5-json":
        ensure => present
    }
}
```

Installing the MySQL module

Because we are going to use the Puppet module for MySQL provided by Puppet Labs, installing the module is very straightforward; we simply add it as a `git` submodule to our project with the following command:

```
git submodule add https://github.com/puppetlabs/puppetlabs-mysql.git provision/modules/mysql
```

 You might want to use a specific release for this module, as the code changes on a semi-regular basis. A stable release is available at https://github.com/puppetlabs/puppetlabs-mysql/releases/tag/3.1.0.

Default manifest

Finally, we need to pull these modules together, and install them when our machine is provisioned. To do this, we simply add the following modules to our `vagrant.pp` manifest file in the `provision/manifests` folder.

Installing Nginx and PHP

We need to include our `nginx` class and optionally provide a filename for the configuration file; if we don't provide one, the default will be used:

```
class {
    'nginx':
        file => 'default'
}
```

Similarly for PHP, we need to include the class and in this case, pass an `nginx` parameter to ensure that it installs PHP5-FPM too:

```
class {
    'php':
        nginx => true
}
```

Hostname configuration

We should tell our Vagrant virtual machine what its hostname is by adding a host resource to our manifest:

```
host { 'lemp-stack.local':
    ip => '127.0.0.1',
    host_aliases => 'localhost',
}
```

E-mail sending services

Because some of our projects might involve sending e-mails, we should install e-mail sending services on our virtual machine. As these are simply two packages, it makes more sense to include them in our Vagrant manifest, as opposed to their own modules:

```
package { "postfix":
    ensure => present
}

package { "mailutils":
    ensure => present
}
```

MySQL configuration

Because the MySQL module is very flexible and manages all aspects of MySQL, there is quite a bit for us to configure. We need to perform the following steps:

1. Create a database.
2. Create a user.
3. Give the user permission to use the database (`grants`).
4. Configure the MySQL root password.
5. Install the MySQL client.
6. Install the MySQL client bindings for PHP.

The MySQL server class has a range of parameters that can be passed to configure it, including databases, users, and grants. So, first, we need to define what the databases, users, and grants are that we want to be configured:

```
$databases = {
  'lemp' => {
    ensure  => 'present',
    charset => 'utf8'
  },
}

$users = {
  'lemp@localhost' => {
    ensure                   => 'present',
    max_connections_per_hour => '0',
    max_queries_per_hour     => '0',
    max_updates_per_hour     => '0',
    max_user_connections     => '0',
    password_hash            => 'MySQL-Password-Hash',
  },
}
```

 The `password_hash` parameter here is for a hash generated by MySQL. You can generate a password hash by connecting to an existing MySQL instance and running a query such as `SELECT PASSWORD('password')`.

A Sample LEMP Stack

The grant maps our user and database and specifies what permissions the user can perform on that database when connecting from a particular host (in this case, localhost—so from the virtual machine itself):

```
$grants = {
  'lemp@localhost/lemp.*' => {
    ensure     => 'present',
    options    => ['GRANT'],
    privileges => ['ALL'],
    table      => 'lemp.*',
    user       => 'lemp@localhost',
  },
}
```

We then pass these values to the MySQL server class. We also provide a root password for MySQL (unlike earlier, this is provided in plain text), and we can override the options from the MySQL configuration file. This is unlike our own Nginx module that provides a full file—in this instance, the MySQL module provides a template configuration file and the changes are replaced in that template to create a configuration file:

```
class { '::mysql::server':
  root_password    => 'lemp-root-password',
  override_options => { 'mysqld' => { 'max_connections' => '1024' } },
  databases => $databases,
  users => $users,
  grants => $grants,
  restart => true
}
```

As we will have a web server running on this machine, which needs to connect to this database server, we also need the client library and the client bindings for PHP, so that we can include them too:

```
include '::mysql::client'

class { '::mysql::bindings':
  php_enable => true
}
```

Launching the virtual machine

In order to launch our new virtual machine, we simply need to run the following command:

`Vagrant up`

As per *Chapter 6, Provisioning Vagrant Machines with Puppet, Ansible, and Chef*, we should now see our VM boot and the various Puppet phases execute. If all goes well, we should see no errors in this process.

Summary

In this chapter, we learned about the steps involved in creating a brand new Vagrant project, configuring it to integrate with our host machine, and setting up a standard LEMP stack using the Puppet provisioning tool. Now you should have a basic understanding of Vagrant and how to use it to ensure that your software projects are managed more effectively!

Index

A

Ansible
  about 56
  books, URL 55
  commands, running 63
  cron module 62
  Galaxy, URL 63
  group module, URL 63
  installing 56, 57
  inventory, creating 57
  modules 58
  operating systems, URL 56
  playbooks 56
  playbooks, creating 58
  provisioning with 83
  roles, using 63
  software, installing 59
  used, for server provision 64, 65
  user module, URL 63
Ansible, file management
  about 60
  file, copying 60, 61
  folders, creating 62
  group module, creating 63
  symlink, creating 61
  user module, creating 63
Ansible software, installing
  nginx package, installing 59
  nginx service, running 60
  package manager, updating 59
apt module
  URL 59
Atlas
  account, URL 114
  box creation form, URL 114
  boxes, discovering 112
  boxes, distributing 114-116
  boxes, URL 112
  connecting with 116
  existing boxes, updating 113
  features 111
  new boxes, installing 113
  outdated boxes, checking for 113
  sharing with 116
  URL 111
  Vagrant, connecting to
    Vagrant Cloud 116, 117
  Vagrant virtual machine, connecting to 119
  Vagrant virtual machine, sharing over
    HTTP(S) 117, 118
  Vagrant virtual machine,
    sharing to 119, 120
authentication, Vagrant
  about 107
  admin group 107
  sudoers file 107, 108
  user group 107

C

Chef
  about 67, 68
  Chef-solo, using 84
  commands, running 74, 75
  common resource functionalities 76
  cookbooks, creating with 68
  cookbooks, using 77
  cron resource type, managing 74
  groups, creating 75
  groups, managing 75
  installing 109

on Vagrant, provisioning with 83
recipes, creating with 68
resources 69
roles, URL 84
run anatomy, URL 77
sudoers file, updating 76
URL, for tutorial 77
used, for provisioning servers 77
users, creating 75, 76
users, managing 75
using, in client/server mode 85
Chef, file management
about 71
file, copying 71, 72
folders, creating 73
multiple folders, creating in single process with looping 73
symlink, creating 72
Chef Infrastructure Automation Cookbook
URL 67
Chef, resource types
cron 69
execute 69
file 69
group 69
package 69
service 69
template 69
URL 69
user 69
Chef, software installing
about 69
nginx package, installing 70
nginx service, running 71
package manager, updating 70
Chef-solo
configuration, URL 77
using 84
commands
autorunning 29, 30
cookbooks
creating, with Chef 68
cron module
URL 62

F

file module
URL 61

G

group module
URL 63
Guest Additions, VirtualBox 106

H

HashiCorp Atlas. *See* **Atlas**
host and guest machine interaction, managing
about 27
networking 28, 29
port forwarding 27
synced folders 28
hostname
configuring 128

I

Instant Chef Starter
URL 67
inventory, Ansible
creating 57

L

Linux, nginx, MySQL and PHP (LEMP) 44, 121

M

manifests
about 128
e-mail sending, services 128
hostname configuration 128
MySQL configuration 129, 130
nginx, installing 128
PHP, installing 128
modules, Ansible
about 58

Apt 58
Copy 58
Git 58
Service 58
URL 58
multimachine project
  destroying 97
multiple provisioners
  using, on single project 86
multiple virtual machines
  connecting, over SSH 91-93
  defining 90
  networking 93-95
  provisioning 95, 96
  using, with Vagrant 90
MySQL
  configuring 129, 130
  installing 127

N

Network File System (NFS) 28
networking 28, 29
nginx
  installing 123-128
notify parameter 42

O

Opscode community site, Chef cookbooks
  URL 77

P

package subcommand 109
parameters 41
PHP
  installing 125-128
port forwarding 27
project
  creating 19-22
provisioners
  about 108
  Chef, installing 109
  Puppet, installing 109
provisioning
  about 36, 37
  overriding, via command line 86

  with Ansible, on Vagrant 82, 83
  with Chef, on Vagrant 83
  with Puppet, on Vagrant 80
  with SSH 85
  with Vagrant 79
provisioning, options
  Ansible 29
  Chef 29
  Puppet 29
  Shell 29
Puppet
  about 37
  blog, URL 82
  books, URL 36
  classes 38
  commands, running 48
  configurable classes, creating 51-53
  cron resource type, managing 48
  default manifests 38-40
  file management 45
  group resource type, managing 49
  idempotent feature 37
  installing 109
  modules 53
  notify parameter 42
  provisioning, in action 81, 82
  provisioning with, on Vagrant 80
  refreshonly parameter 42
  resource 40
  subscribe parameter 42
  sudoers file, updating 50, 51
  URL 82
  used, for creating manifests 38
  used, for creating modules 38
  used, for server provision 53
  user resource type, managing 49, 50
  user resource type, URL 49
  using, in client/server mode 82
  using, in standalone mode 80, 81
Puppet, file management
  about 45
  file, copying 45
  folders, creating 47
  multiple folders, creating 47
  symlink, creating 46
Puppet Forge
  URL 53

Puppet manifests
  creating 123
  MySQL module, installing 127
  nginx, installing 123-125
  PHP, installing 125, 126
  URL 127

Puppet, resources
  executing, in stages 43
  execution, ordering 41
  requisites 41
  types 40
  types, URL 41

Puppet, resource types
  cron 40
  exec 40
  file 40
  group 40
  package 40
  service 40
  user 40

Puppet software, installing
  about 43
  nginx package, installing 44
  nginx service, running 45
  package manager, updating 44

PuTTY
  URL 27

R

recipes, Chef
  creating 68
  URL 77

refreshonly parameter 42

S

servers
  provisioning, Chef used 77

SSH
  multiple virtual machines, connecting to 91-93
  provisioning with 85

standalone mode
  Puppet using 80, 81

subscribe parameter 42

sudoers file
  about 107, 108
  URL 107

supervisord
  about 39
  URL 38

supervisor module
  URL 39

symlink
  creating 46

synced folders 28

T

template module
  URL 60

U

user module
  URL 63

V

Vagrant
  about 8, 33
  authentication 107
  configuration file 9
  documentation, URL 100
  download page 15
  installing 15-17
  multiple virtual machines, using 90
  new base box, URL 100
  project, creating 19-22, 121, 122
  provisioning, options 30
  provisioning with 79
  provisioning, with Chef 83
  provisioning, with Puppet 80
  requisites 10
  URL 8, 10, 27
  Vagrant-controlled guest machines, controlling 22
  VirtualBox, installing 11-15
  virtual machine, powering up 23, 24
  virtual machine, resuming 25
  virtual machine setup, approaches 35

virtual machine, shutting down 25
virtual machine, suspending 24
Vagrant authentication
    insecure private key pair 108
    insecure public key pair 108
Vagrant boxes
    adding 31
    add subcommand 31
    current environments box, updating 33
    listing 32
    list subcommand 31, 32
    managing 30, 31
    outdated subcommand 31, 32
    remove subcommand 31, 32
    removing 32
    repackage subcommand 31-33
    repackaging 33
    updates, checking for 32
    update subcommand 31-33
Vagrant boxes, Atlas
    discovering 112
    distributing 114-116
    existing boxes, updating 113
    new boxes, installing 112
    outdated boxes, checking for 113
Vagrant Cloud. *See* **Atlas**
Vagrant virtual machine, Atlas
    sharing, over HTTP(S) 117, 118
VirtualBox
    installing 11-15
    machine, preparing 100-106
virtual machine (VM)
    cleaning up 109
    launching 131
virtual machine, Vagrant-controlled
    connecting to, over SSH 27
    managing 22
    off Vagrantfile changes, updating 26
    powering up 23
    resuming 25
    shutting down 25
    starting, from scratch 25
    suspending 24

Y

Yaml Ain't Markup Language (YAML) 56

[PACKT] PUBLISHING

Thank you for buying
Creating Development Environments with Vagrant
Second Edition

About Packt Publishing

Packt, pronounced 'packed', published its first book, *Mastering phpMyAdmin for Effective MySQL Management*, in April 2004, and subsequently continued to specialize in publishing highly focused books on specific technologies and solutions.

Our books and publications share the experiences of your fellow IT professionals in adapting and customizing today's systems, applications, and frameworks. Our solution-based books give you the knowledge and power to customize the software and technologies you're using to get the job done. Packt books are more specific and less general than the IT books you have seen in the past. Our unique business model allows us to bring you more focused information, giving you more of what you need to know, and less of what you don't.

Packt is a modern yet unique publishing company that focuses on producing quality, cutting-edge books for communities of developers, administrators, and newbies alike. For more information, please visit our website at www.packtpub.com.

About Packt Open Source

In 2010, Packt launched two new brands, Packt Open Source and Packt Enterprise, in order to continue its focus on specialization. This book is part of the Packt Open Source brand, home to books published on software built around open source licenses, and offering information to anybody from advanced developers to budding web designers. The Open Source brand also runs Packt's Open Source Royalty Scheme, by which Packt gives a royalty to each open source project about whose software a book is sold.

Writing for Packt

We welcome all inquiries from people who are interested in authoring. Book proposals should be sent to author@packtpub.com. If your book idea is still at an early stage and you would like to discuss it first before writing a formal book proposal, then please contact us; one of our commissioning editors will get in touch with you.

We're not just looking for published authors; if you have strong technical skills but no writing experience, our experienced editors can help you develop a writing career, or simply get some additional reward for your expertise.

[PACKT] open source
community experience distilled
PUBLISHING

Configuration Management with Chef-Solo

ISBN: 978-1-78398-246-2   Paperback: 116 pages

A comprehensive guide to get you up and running with Chef-Solo

1. Explore various techniques that will help you save time in Infrastructure management.

2. Use the power of Chef-Solo to run your servers and configure and deploy applications in an automated manner.

3. This book will help you to understand the need for the configuration management tool and provides you with a step-by-step guide to maintain your existing infrastructure.

OpenStack Cloud Computing Cookbook
Second Edition

ISBN: 978-1-78216-758-7   Paperback: 396 pages

Over 100 recipes to successfully set up and manage your OpenStack cloud environments with complete coverage of Nova, Swift, Keystone, Glance, Horizon, Neutron, and Cinder

1. Updated for OpenStack Grizzly.

2. Learn how to install, configure, and manage all of the OpenStack core projects including new topics like block storage and software defined networking.

3. Learn how to build your Private Cloud utilizing DevOps and Continuous Integration tools and techniques.

Please check **www.PacktPub.com** for information on our titles

Rapid Ghost [Video]

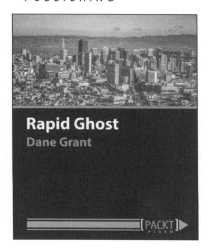

ISBN: 978-1-78355-299-3   Duration: 01:23 hours

Experience effortless blogging with Ghost

1. Create attractive blogs using the amazing new blogging platform.
2. Configure and customize your Ghost blog using custom themes and add-ons.
3. Get a better understanding of Ghost by setting up your own blog with easy-to-follow instructions.

Performance Testing with JMeter 2.9

ISBN: 978-1-78216-584-2   Paperback: 148 pages

Learn how to test web applications using Apache JMeter with practical, hands-on examples

1. Create realistic and maintainable scripts for web applications.
2. Use various JMeter components to achieve testing goals.
3. Removal of unnecessary errors and code compilation.
4. Acquire skills that will enable you to leverage the cloud for distributed testing.

Please check **www.PacktPub.com** for information on our titles